OUT OF STYLE

OUT OF STYLE

Reanimating Stylistic Study in Composition and Rhetoric

PAUL BUTLER

UTAH STATE UNIVERSITY PRESS
Logan, Utah
2008

Utah State University Press
Logan, Utah 84322–7800

ISBN: 978-0-87421-679-0 (paper)
ISBN: 978-0-87421-680-6 (e-book)

Manufactured in the United States of America.
Cover design by Barbara Yale-Read.
Library of Congress Cataloging-in-Publication Data Library of Congress Cataloging-in-Publication Data

Butler, Paul,
Out of style : reanimating stylistic study in composition and rhetoric / Paul Butler.
p. cm.
Includes bibliographical references and index.
ISBN 978-0-87421-679-0 (pbk. : alk. paper)
1. Language and languages–Style. 2. Rhetoric. I. Title.
P301.B79 2008
808'.042–dc22

2007041720

To
Joan L. Baxter (Mrs. B.)

In memory of
Shirley B. Butler

CONTENTS

ACKNOWLEDGMENTS

On a recent summer morning, unable to write in my office because a fire had disabled a transformer on campus and cut power to most of the university, I piled approximately twenty books and my laptop computer into the backseat of my car and headed to the Truckee Book and Bean, near Lake Tahoe, California. As I pulled onto I-80, the main east-west route in the area, a sign said the town of Truckee was just nineteen miles from my home in northwest Reno, with all but a few of those miles across the California border. Along the way, I passed through some of the West's most scenic terrain, with Truckee the first leg in a route that ascends through the Tahoe National Forest and Donner Pass before eventually descending into Sacramento and San Francisco. The Book and Bean, which I had discovered earlier in the summer after a colleague suggested it, is one of a handful of coffeehouses or similar venues that have seen me through the writing and revising process of this book. For those like me who do our best work in public spaces, it is gratifying to know that the European café tradition is alive and well in the American coffeehouse, whatever shape or vision that takes in different locations. For me, those spaces include, roughly in chronological order, Borders in Syracuse; Space Untitled (now Pomegranate) and the Reading Room of the New York Public Library in Manhattan; Baker Boys and Basic in Jersey City; Barnes and Noble, Bibo, Borders, and Walden's Coffeehouse in Reno; and the Book and Bean. I appreciate the cheerful reception I received in all these places and the long, uninterrupted hours I spent at their small and large open tables with laptop in hand.

Along with these scenes of writing, I would also like to acknowledge the institutional spaces that informed the writing of this book. While grounded in theory rather than pedagogy,

Out of Style's origins clearly benefited from the teaching of a number of fine professors in composition and rhetoric. First, I thank those with whom I was privileged to study at Syracuse University: Collin Brooke, Fred Gale, Xin Liu Gale, Margaret Himley, Becky Howard, Louise Wetherbee Phelps, Kendall Phillips, Eileen Schell, Catherine Smith, Gay Washburn, and Jim Zebroski; at the University of Arizona: Theresa Enos and Roxanne Mountford; and at the University of Louisiana, Lafayette: Ann Dobie and Jim McDonald. Without the help of several extraordinary mentors at Syracuse, this book could not have come to fruition, and in that regard I thank Collin Brooke, Dana Harrington, and Jim Zebroski for patient, productive, and wise counsel that always exceeded my expectations. Jim continued to offer unfailing encouragement through a process that he often, and appropriately, described as a "marathon." I am particularly indebted to Louise Wetherbee Phelps, a scholar whose dedication to and passion for the study of style opened up a treasure trove of understanding through the incredible knowledge and wisdom she generously shared with me. As scholars and teachers of composition and rhetoric, we too often wonder about the impact we have on students' lives, and I want to affirm here the power of teaching to make a difference; teachers have made an important difference in my life.

My trajectory in completing this book has certainly been aided by a number of fine colleagues in a profession I feel thankful every day to have found. To that end I thank my talented and supportive former colleagues at Montclair State University, especially First-Year Writing Director Emily Isaacs, Laura Nicosia, and Jessica Restaino. At the University of Nevada, Reno, I am fortunate to work with a superb group of colleagues in rhetoric and composition and more generally in writing studies: Kathy Boardman, Shane Borrowman, Chris Coake, Jane Detweiler, Christine Norris, Gailmarie Pahmeier, Susan Palwick, Mark Waldo, and Mary Webb. I am grateful to the many other English Department colleagues who have offered support during the year, especially Michael Branch, Joe Calabrese,

Cathryn Donohue, Marilee Dupree, David Fenimore, Valerie Fridland, Justin Gifford, Cheryll Glotfelty, Don Hardy, Ann Keniston, James Mardock, Eric Rasmussen, and Ann Ronald. I am indebted to three individuals who do much to help the entire department and who offered great assistance during this undertaking: Cami Allen, Alec Ausbrooks, and Michelle Beaty. I thank Dean Heather Hardy for her generous support and the Scholarly and Creative Activities Grants Program of the College of Liberal Arts. In addition, I am grateful to colleague Jen Hill, who encouraged me in my SCAGP application and, in particular, to English Department Chair Stacy Burton, whose support for faculty and dedicated stewardship of the department make her an unusually visionary leader. I am also extremely grateful to Amy March and Sarah Perrault, doctoral students in rhetoric and composition at the University of Nevada, Reno, who read my work with extraordinary care and insight and offered highly intelligent editorial comments that helped me improve my manuscript.

I would also like to thank a number of individuals in the field whose support has made a difference in my ability to complete this book. For their feedback on my work, I owe a debt of gratitude to Janice Lauer and Duane Roen, who read a version of chapter four in preparation for its publication in *Rhetoric Review*. I thank *Rhetoric Review* editor Theresa Enos for supporting my work and the Taylor and Francis Group LLC for permission to reproduce that article as part of chapter four. I am indebted to the two anonymous readers for Utah State University Press who offered incredibly helpful and prescient suggestions on revising my manuscript and in the process enabled me to write a much better book. I also thank Richard Leo Enos of Texas Christian University, who gave knowledgeable and generous advice on an early version of the historical account I provide in chapter two. His suggestions opened up many new scholarly sources and avenues for me to pursue. At Utah State University Press, I thank Michael Spooner for his patient, helpful, and enthusiastic support of this book. He has offered the kind of encouragement that anyone undertaking a project of this scope would welcome and appreciate.

The book has benefited from friends in the field whose good will has bolstered me during the long hours. In particular, I thank Susan Adams, Lindal Buchanan, Tracy Hamler Carrick, Risa Gorelick, Tobi Jacobi, Seth Kahn, Deanya Lattimore, Brad Lucas, Nancy Mack, Joddy Murray, Mary Queen, Amy Robillard, Brooke Rollins, Bonnie Selting, and Joseph J. Williams. I also thank my students, graduate and undergraduate, who have helped make my work fascinating and enjoyable. Outside composition, I thank Michael Clarke, Aaron Dalenburg, Carl Landorno, Bev Lassiter, Lee Medina, Scott Sutherland, Pete and Wendy Tomco, and Diana Wilson Wing.

To the circle of friends who have offered so much during this project I add family members who have provided tremendous help and encouragement through the years: I am grateful to Robert Butler, who is always interested in talking about the life of scholars and teachers, and Tod and Katie Butler, who give me a much-needed refuge at their Anchorage "homestead" as well constant support for my efforts. I also thank Matt and Aislinn Butler Hetterman; Chris, Pacey, and Jaida Butler Harris; Josh, Liz, and Koda Butler; Ann and John Osborn; Ken Fleshman and Vicki Maddox; Carolyn, Jim, and Amei Gove; Barb Fleshman and Bill and Nathan White; and Sally Butler. The book is dedicated to the memory of Shirley Butler, who always believed in my ability to achieve whatever goals I set for myself.

Finally, I dedicate the book to Joan L. Baxter, affectionately known as Mrs. B., a committed and gifted teacher who always said she believed that teaching and writing were my natural inclinations and showed me how they can make a difference in others' lives. In a culture that doesn't seem to admire teaching or the life of the mind very much, we are fortunate to have exemplary individuals like Joan Baxter who remind us daily of the real values that sustain us.

Reno, Nevada
January 2008

OUT OF STYLE

1

INTRODUCTION
Reanimating Style in Composition and Rhetoric

OVERVIEW: STYLE AND LANGUAGE

As a student in the French School at Middlebury College, I wrote a stylistic analysis of nineteenth-century French poet José-María de Heredia's sonnet (1978, 117), "Les Conquérants" ("The Conquistadores"), completely unaware at the time that the study of style is part of a rhetorical tradition that began more than 2,500 years ago. Examining the poem from several perspectives—phonological (sound and rhythm), syntactic, lexical, semantic, and rhetorical—I looked at such features as the poet's use of explosive consonants and stops (including enjambment) as devices to convey the harshness of the conqueror's "brutal" departure; the later contrast with certain liquid and nasal consonants and the repetition of assonant vowel sounds to signal a shift in mood after the discovery of an exotic new land; the poet's reversal of syntax, first to speed up and then to slow down the rhythm of the poem; the sonnet's changing lexical field, with an opposition between nouns with masculine and feminine genders that parallels the poem's increasingly ameliorative movement from conquest to hopeful acceptance; and the contrastive use of rhyme to reflect the imprisonment of the conquerors who, literally and figuratively, break away from their native country to an alluring new world. While analyzing the poem's stylistic features and patterns, I was able to demonstrate how Heredia deployed various elements of form to help achieve his overall effect. I now know that my analysis of the sonnet falls under the rubric of stylistics—or the study of style—whose history in literature complements its ancient counterpart in the history of rhetoric and its equally dynamic history in the field of composition.

In composition studies, the salient features of style—which Richard Ohmann defines as "a way of writing" (1967, 135)—are often different from those in literature, and the texts examined are generally non-literary prose rather than poetry or fiction. Like literary stylistics, however, composition's approach to style has clearly been influenced by linguistics, the study and description of language phenomena in units up to and including the sentence, and by rhetoric, the study and use of language in context to inform, persuade, and produce knowledge. Some of the linguistic and rhetorical features I examined in Heredia's sonnet include sound and rhythm, vocabulary, diction, register, syntax, and semantics, as well as figures of speech like tropes (e.g., metaphor) and schemes (e.g., parallelism). Although various other elements (e.g., phonetics and graphics) are also relevant to style, I argue that stylistic features are part of descriptive and interpretive frameworks—from classical rhetoric, discourse analysis, linguistics, and literary theory, history, and criticism, for example—that link their objects of study to the ways one goes about studying them.

Depending on what aspect of a stylistic relationship is being emphasized, one of several definitions of style might be used, each one representing a different theoretical approach to the topic. Indeed, it is fair to say that any definition of style involves one of several long-standing debates that have informed the study of the canon throughout history. Thus, for example, when Ohmann defines style as "a way of writing," he is taking the position that style is a choice (of words, syntax, etc.) a writer makes among alternative forms. His broader argument is that style (or form) is separate from content (or meaning), and for him this "dualistic" theory underpins a central question: "If style does not have to do with *ways* of saying *something* . . . is there anything at all which is worth naming 'style?'" (Ohmann 1959, 2). While this perennial form-content issue is discussed in detail below, its brief mention here is intended to indicate the complexity surrounding the question of what constitutes "style." The counterpart to Ohmann's dualistic view of style is an "organic" position, often attributed to Aristotle, asserting that form and content are inseparable. Another definition of style—the unique expression of an individual's personality ("style is the man")—raises the question of whether style is an unconscious process or a matter of conscious control among writers (Milic 1971, 77). Defining style as a unique or idiosyncratic—sometimes, an extraordinary—use of language implies an opposing norm or a standard, ordinary use that raises theoretical debates about whether to identify style with social groups or with characteristics of an individual's personality. Still another question focuses on whether style is measured subjectively, by so-called impressionistic techniques, or objectively, through the application of quantitative measurements, especially computers.

Because these multiple—and often competing—definitions of style are sometimes confusing, I define style as the deployment of rhetorical resources, in written discourse, to create and express meaning. According to this definition, style involves the use of written language features as habitual patterns, rhetorical options, and conscious choices at the sentence and word level (see Connors 1997, 257), even though the *effects* of these features extend to broader areas of discourse and beyond. The term "rhetorical," while informed by a rich history in oral discourse, refers specifically to written language as it is used to inform, persuade, and generate knowledge for different purposes, occasions, and audiences. This definition not only accommodates several perspectives on language, but also accounts for ways in which language theories can aid the deployment of style in various contexts. While I am adopting a rhetorical definition of style that includes qualities like tone, emphasis, and irony, certain linguistic concepts are also relevant. For example, some of the phenomena I used to analyze Heredia's poem (e.g., diction and syntax) are linguistic as well as rhetorical. However, as Sharon Crowley argues in "Linguistics and Composition" (1989), the use of linguistics in the study of style is problematic in that "American linguistics habitually privileged the spoken over the written word" (492) and thereby avoided the more complex structures used, for instance, by professional writers. Furthermore, Crowley acknowledges the general deficiency of linguistics as an organizing system: "To date, no linguistically based stylistic taxonomy has appeared that begins to rival the scope of that developed . . . by classical rhetoricians" (491). In addition, Susan Peck MacDonald asserts that "one of the unfortunate disciplinary accidents of the late twentieth-century period is that trends in linguistics have been out of synch with English" (MacDonald 2007, 609).

For my purposes, then, I am focusing on the features of style that can be described locally through rhetoric, even though the effects of those elements are not necessarily local, but extend to more global features of discourse or to readers' responses (see Williams 2005, 351). One example of a language phenomenon that functions precisely in this way is the concept of "cohesion," which M. A. K. Halliday and Ruqaiya Hasan define as the "relations of meaning that exist within the text, and that define it as a text" (1976, 4). Even though cohesion can be described locally—for example, the cohesive device "exophora," or the use of pronouns that have an antecedent in a previous sentence, is a device occurring within individual sentences—it is manifested only globally, or throughout a text, where it refers to the relational effects of the pronoun use, or what the authors call "non-structural text-forming relations" (7). As Stephen Witte and Lester Faigley explain in "Coherence, Cohesion, and Writing Quality," "For Halliday and Hasan, cohesion depends upon lexical and grammatical relationships that allow sentence sequences to be understood as connected discourse rather than as autonomous sentences" (Witte and Faigley 1997, 214). Louise Wetherbee Phelps adds that cohesion, as used in composition, "has been reserved for stylistic features of texts (language) in global contrast to their semantic and pragmatic aspects of structures (meaning)" (1988, 174). In *Cohesion in English* (1976), a book that had a profound impact on composition studies when it appeared,

Halliday and Hasan explain further how cohesion passes from language into meaning and discourse structure:

> The concept of cohesion is set up to account for relations in discourse . . . without the implication that there is some structural unit that is above the sentence. Cohesion refers to the range of possibilities that exist for linking something with what has gone before. Since this linking is achieved through relations in meaning . . . what is in question is the set of meaning relations which function in this way: the semantic resources which are drawn on for the purpose of creating text. (10)

In acknowledging, as Halliday and Hasan do, that stylistic effects extend to patterns of meaning beyond sentences, I contend nonetheless that efforts to attribute linguistic features to discourse, sometimes called "text linguistics," have been unsuccessful. For example, scholars like Francis Christensen attempted to devise a rhetoric (or grammar) of the paragraph analogous to a sentence-based model. In "A Generative Rhetoric of the Paragraph," Christensen argued that "the principles used [in his article 'A Generative Rhetoric of the Sentence'] were no less applicable to the paragraph" (1978, 76). Yet, composition scholars like Paul Rodgers (1966) rejected Christensen's "sentence-expanding" notion of "the average paragraph as a 'macro-sentence or meta-sentence,'" because he felt that the principles were not transferable. Similarly, Rodgers critiqued what he called Alton Becker's attempt "to analyze paragraphs 'by extending grammatical theories now used in analyzing and describing sentence structure'" (73). In addition, W. Ross Winterowd ultimately "emphatically repudiated" his own previous contention that "the sentence is the most productive analogical model for exploration of 'grammar' beyond the sentence" (1986, 245). Similarly, Frank D'Angelo's (1976) effort to extend syntactic structures to larger stretches of discourse—one he attempted to develop into a "full-fledged theory and pedagogy of composition" (Crowley 1989, 496)—was never taken up broadly by scholars in the discipline.

For similar reasons, I argue that style is not the equivalent of literary studies' "thematics" or its theory of "textual comparison" (Todorov 1971, 36), which attempts to apply stylistic features to whole bodies of work. Part of the reason for moving away from text linguistics came about with the understanding that language does not *itself* create or express meaning and that a great deal of what makes meaning is contextual and dependent on such "extralinguistic" factors as the reader and his or her responses to the text. In his analysis of a recently translated essay on style and pedagogy by Mikhail M. Bakhtin (see Bazerman 2005, 333–38), Joseph M. Williams explains the importance of these types of responses:

> Most of the words we use to describe style displace our responses to a text into that text or its writer. When we say a sentence is clear, we mean that we understand it easily. When we say a speaker is coherent, we mean that we have no trouble following him or her. Such qualities are neither in the speaker ("You are clear") nor in the speaker's language ("Your sentence is clear"). They are in our responses to particular syntactic, lexical, and other features on the page (or in the air), uttered or written and heard or read in a particular context. (Williams 2005, 351)[1]

Given the importance of our responses to numerous textual and non-textual features, it is clear that stretches of discourse beyond the sentence—what Rodgers, to cite one example, called a "stadium of discourse" (1966, 73)—reveal other important insights into language and meaning related to stylistic analysis. For example, in a slightly different approach, Winston Weathers attempted to define style more broadly in his article, "Grammars of Style" (1990). A "grammar of style," he suggested, is the "set of conventions governing the construction of a whole composition; the criteria by which a writer selects the stylistic materials, method of organization and development, compositional pattern and structure he is to use in preparing any particular composition." Weathers's argument that style includes the "conventions . . . of a whole composition" (201) influenced some scholars who reconceived of style as arrangement, as in the Weathers-inspired collection *Elements of Alternate Style* (Bishop 1997). This approach, in fact, is suggestive of Young, Becker, and Pike's contention that style is part of the "universe of discourse," an idea they developed in their innovative text *Rhetoric: Discovery and Change* (1970).

THE BREADTH OF STYLISTIC INTEREST IN STYLE'S "GOLDEN AGE"

I argue that composition has developed a selective and biased memory of what I call the "Golden Age" of style study, roughly a three-decade period (from the 1960s to the mid-1980s) that overlaps with what is commonly known today as the "process movement." As evidence of this claim, I cite recent works that express renewed interest in the study of style during that time period, yet conceive of it narrowly—primarily as syntax. Two examples are Robert Connors's article "The Erasure of the Sentence" (2000) in which he discusses so-called "sentence rhetorics" (121), largely based in syntax, that he says disappeared around 1985: generative rhetoric, sentence combining, and imitation; and Crowley's article surveying linguistics and pedagogies of style from 1950 to 1980, where she suggests that in both structural linguistics and the transformational linguistics practice of sentence combining, the basis for the study of style was the use of "syntactic structures in English" (1989, 487). During the process era, Winterowd designated as "pedagogical stylistics" (1975, 253) the practical applications of largely syntactic methods that some considered the most useful for effecting improvement in student writing.

While it is true that syntax was a prominent focus of style study during the Golden Age, it certainly was not the exclusive focus, and the tendency to read other stylistic features out of accounts of that era reinforces composition's increasingly selective memory of it. What's more, the limited recollection adds fuel to today's nearly universal characterization of style as a "remnant" of current-traditional rhetoric, as the rhetorical antithesis of invention (see Chap. 3), and as focused on what some scholars, borrowing from Connors, refer to as "sentence-based pedagogies" (96). If, as I argue, the study of style during the Golden Age was not limited to a narrow focus on syntax or its use in developing syntactic maturity in student writing, then what did style studies, broadly construed, consist of during a period of composition history that overlapped with the discipline's process movement? Furthermore, what would a complete inventory of these stylistic practices comprise today? To answer that question fully, it is necessary to conduct historical research of the process era and Golden Age that goes beyond the scope of this book. Nonetheless, by pointing to some of the work that comprised the study of style at the time, I hope to give a sense of the future possibilities that exist for stylistic research, theory, and practice.

In addition to sentence combining and generative rhetoric, many scholars of the Golden Age (and process era) examined theories of cohesion—or the linking of one part of a text to another by means of such devices as reference, substitution, ellipsis, lexical cohesion, and conjunction (Halliday and Hasan 1976)—and coherence, the ability of interpreters to discover and attribute holistic meanings to texts, cued by cohesive systems (Phelps 1988, 174). One example of work on cohesion during the Golden Age was Young and Becker's "lexical equivalence chains," high-level sequences of discourse, which they discussed in an essay on the contributions of tagmemic rhetoric to composition, especially stylistic study (1967, 99–100). A similar area of study involved what has been variously described in different traditions as "topic and comment," "theme and rheme," or the "known and new" contract, which posits that a sentence conveys its message most cohesively if the "topic," or theme of the sentence, contains the "known" or least important information and precedes the "comment," which expresses the "new" or most important information related to the theme (Vande Kopple 1990, 215). The various terms for this theory can be confusing, as Phelps points out, because "it is not clear whether we are dealing with different labels for a few functions or many different functions" (1984, 52). This umbrella of terms was often grouped under the rubric of what William Vande Kopple has called "Functional Sentence Perspective (FSP)" (1990) and was used in the work of such composition scholars as Joseph Williams (1994) and E. D. Hirsch (1977). Phelps (1984, 52) suggests, however, that some of the originators of the terms included Halliday (1967), Wallace Chafe (1973), George Dillon (1981), and such Prague School linguists as Frantisek Daneš (1974).

In addition to an interest in cohesion and coherence, some scholars focused on the difference between "nominal" and "verbal" styles; nominalization generally refers to producing a noun by adding derivational affixes to a verb or adjective (e.g., proficient and proficiency). Williams and Rosemary Hake found in a series of studies that an essay written in a nominal style "tends to be perceived as better organized, better supported, and better argued than the corresponding verbal paper" (1986, 178–79). The preference for nominalization among high school and some college composition instructors, however, contravenes Williams's contention that "sentences seem clearer when actions are verbs," though he does acknowledge the usefulness of nominalization as a cohesive device (Williams 1994, 38, 48). Another area of stylistic study based on readers' perceptions of the readability of writing hails from the field of psycholinguistics. In *The Philosophy of Composition* (1977), Hirsch introduced the idea of the "relative readability" of prose, which is the idea of improving style based on Herbert Spencer's (1881) concepts of "economizing the reader's or hearer's attention" and the "least possible mental effort" (11) . Building on Spencer's ideas, Hirsch went on to define relative readability as follows: "*Assuming that two texts convey the same meaning, the more readable text will take less time and effort to understand*" (85; emphasis original). Even though Hirsch later disavowed the concept of relative readability, it represented one area of stylistic attention influenced by psychology during that era.

In addition to the predominately syntactic areas of sentence combining and generative rhetoric, there was also widespread interest in rhetorical imitation. While imitation certainly involves syntactic features (see Connors 2000), it also goes beyond that rhetorical aspect of sentences. Frank Farmer and Phillip Arrington (1993) have defined imitation as "the approximation, whether conscious or unconscious, of exemplary models, whether textual, behavioral, or human, for the expressed goal of improved student writing" (13). The practice draws on many traditions going back to such classical rhetoricians as Gorgias, Isocrates, Cicero, and Quintilian. In evaluating the ideas of some of these Sophistic and Roman rhetors, Mary Minock suggests in "Toward a Postmodern Pedagogy of Imitation" (1995) that their concepts of imitation, in a nod to postmodernism, "*echo* some of the insights of Bakhtin, Derrida, and Lacan." Minock goes on to argue that the work of these latter, twentieth-century theorists departs "from the pedagogies of imitation of the past that worked well (only) in their particular contexts" (493). Today, as Farmer and Arrington explain, a direct correlation is often imputed between imitation and a concern for improving stylistic quality: "Since imitation's fortunes have traditionally been wedded to style," they observe, "a good case can be made that a diminished respect for style as an intellectual concern is likewise a narrowing of the possible uses of imitation in the classroom" (15). Thus, Farmer and Arrington argue convincingly that imitation has suffered the same fate as style, is inextricably linked to style, and, like stylistic study, has moved to the periphery in composition studies.

In contrast with the apparent recent demise of imitation (Farmer and Arrington 1993; Connors 2000), during the Golden Age a number of individuals studied the impact of imitation on improving student writing, including Edward P. J. Corbett, whose article "The Theory and Practice of Imitation in Classical Rhetoric" (1989b) is certainly linked to the multiple editions of his textbook *Classical Rhetoric for the Modern Student* (1971). In a book devoted to imitative practice, *Copy and Compose*, Weathers and Otis Winchester (1969) asked students to reproduce model sentences and paragraphs written by professional writers. In her classic text *Forming/Thinking/ Writing: The Composing Imagination,* Ann Berthoff (1982), borrowing from an idea by Phyllis Brooks (1973), introduced the "persona paraphrase" as a means to compose sentences "so that the interaction of syntax and meaning can be observed." With the persona paraphrase, students used a prose passage as a model to guide them in constructing a sequence of sentences that are syntactically close to the model, even though the subject matter of the imitation often varied in significant ways. The result, Berthoff suggested, is that "the model acts to shape your sentences, somewhat the way an armature provides a framework when you are modeling a clay figure" (223). Other compositionists who focused on imitative practices during this era include Winterowd, D'Angelo, and Richard Lanham. Williams and Hake, reporting the results of their experiment, suggested that the use of imitation produces results superior to those of sentence combining in improving students' syntactic fluency (1986, 186–91).

Clearly, the study of style during the Golden Age also included scholarship in other areas not always placed under the rubric of stylistic analysis. For example, some scholars of spelling, following the Chomskyan school, argued that English spelling, far from being random, exhibits logic and can be taught most effectively using a "list" approach based on a "direct" teaching method, which challenged older views that assumed English spelling is fundamentally illogical (Beggs 1984, 319–24). A similar debate evolved over "direct" versus "indirect" pedagogical methods for vocabulary development. Although vocabulary learning was thought to encompass either a semantic or an etymological approach, Mary Moran claimed that "in actuality the two methods are often used in conjunction" (1984, 364). In addition, in a famous study, Charles Read (1971) suggested that preschool children have unconscious knowledge of certain aspects of the sound system in English. Echoing trends that have recently been reprised (see Mann 2003), process-era scholars also studied the role of punctuation in composition, drawing on rhetorical, grammatical, and typographical traditions. Greta

Little (1984) pointed out, however, that despite a wealth of available material, scholars during the Golden Age generally did not treat the study of punctuation as a serious research topic but instead considered it a "peripheral issue of correct usage" that focused on checking the manuscript for mechanical errors. "Thus punctuation," she concluded, "has become associated with the product, having little or no serious role in the writing process" (390).

Another area of style that scholars examined during the Golden Age was usage, defined as "the study of the propriety or, more often, the lack of propriety in using various elements of language" (Ching 1984, 399; see Pooley 1976). Scholars of the era also examined semantic shifts in word formation, lexicography, language variation, and the effects of linguistics and pedagogy, and one result of this scholarship was the Conference on College Composition and Communication's publication "Students' Right to Their Own Language" (1974). In addition to the Students' Right document, works such as Anne Ruggles Gere and Eugene Smith's *Attitudes, Language, and Change* (1979) attempted to change prevailing attitudes and judgments about usage, including ideas about style. Moving beyond usage to the study of meaning, or semantics, some scholars looked at the intersection of style and meaning. In her widely admired book *The Making of Meaning: Metaphors, Models, and Maxims for Writing Teachers,* Berthoff (1981) explored what she calls the "interpretive paraphrase" as "a means why which meanings are hypothesized, identified, developed, modified, discarded, or stabilized" (72). Berthoff goes on to explain that the interpretive paraphrase, as a method of critical inquiry, is a way for writers to ask, "How does it change the meaning if I put it this way?" Berthoff's heuristic has resonated in composition studies in significant ways since her text was published.

Whatever the reason for the demise of interest in the broad study of style after the process era, its neglect in composition studies today points to the exigency I present: If we view "style" as a set of language resources for writers to exploit, then the general absence of style in the field has arguably deprived writers and teachers of an important reservoir of conscious knowledge about these resources and how to cultivate them. It is important to recuperate stylistic theory and practice in composition because they offer untapped tools to writers and teachers. In abandoning this important arena of study, the field has lost theoretical knowledge of the systems underlying stylistic resources, practical knowledge about how writers learn to deploy them, and the potential value of that knowledge for composition practice and pedagogy. I argue that the study of style stands at a liminal moment in composition and rhetoric today, a time when its rediscovery offers great promise to the field. In 2000, *College Composition and Communication* published "The Erasure of the Sentence," in which Connors questions the disappearance of sentence rhetorics from composition theory and pedagogy after 1980 and makes the claim that their marginalization was the result of "a growing wave of anti-formalism, anti-behaviorism, and anti-empiricism" (96). For all practical purposes, Connors's article marks the beginning of a tangible re-emergence of important discussions about the role of style in the discipline.

In the aftermath of Connors's "Erasure," a number of other articles appeared, such as Sharon Myers's "ReMembering the Sentence" (2003), Mann's "Point Counterpoint: Teaching Punctuation as Information Management" (2003), Laura Micciche's article, "Making a Case for Rhetorical Grammar" (2004), Mike Duncan's *College English* piece, "Whatever Happened to the Paragraph?" (2007), and MacDonald's "The Erasure of Language" (2007), published in *CCC*. Broadening the context of the discussion through books and edited collections were Kathryn Flannery's *The Emperor's New Clothes: Literature, Literacy, and the Ideology of Style* (1995), which briefly reinvigorated the question of the ideologies of plain style; *Elements of Alternate Style* (Bishop 1997), inspired largely by Winston Weathers's ideas on "Grammar B" and alternate style from a 1976 essay; the edited collection *Alt Dis: Alternative*

Discourses and the Academy (Shroeder, Fox, and Bizzell 2002); T. R. Johnson's *A Rhetoric of Pleasure: Prose Style and Today's Composition Classroom* (2003); and Johnson and Tom Pace's *Refiguring Prose Style: Possibilities for Writing Pedagogy* (2005). While composition as a discipline may have recently expressed some renewed interest in style, it seems safe to say that, since around 1985, the field as a whole has largely ignored style as part of its theory and practice. Paradoxically, just as composition has turned away from serious stylistic inquiry, other areas of society and culture have often embraced style theory and practice with almost unprecedented interest.

THE SHIFT AWAY FROM STYLE IN COMPOSITION

In his 1976 essay "Linguistics and Composition," Winterowd surveyed the prevailing linguistic and stylistic scholarship that informed both theory and practice in composition studies at that time. Winterowd's essay was part of Gary Tate's *Teaching Composition: Ten Bibliographic Essays* (1976), an edited collection in which several authors linked style in important ways to the then-evolving process movement in composition. Winterowd took up the influence of Chomsky's transformational linguistics, of Christensen's generative grammar, and of the practices of imitation, sentence combining, and sentence composing; Corbett surveyed various "Approaches to the Study of Style"; Richard Larson looked beyond the sentence level to "Structure and Form in Non-Fiction Prose"; and Richard Young related invention to style through Christensen's generative rhetoric and other methods in "Invention: A Topographical Survey." Tate's publication was part of style's Golden Age. The wealth of work produced during this three-decade period amounted to a resurgence of interest in a variety of language-centered methods such as sentence combining, imitation, and generative rhetoric as well as renewed affiliations with classical rhetoric and other disciplines.

Accompanying this renaissance of style was the belief, evident in Tate's edited collection, that its theoretical underpinnings in linguistics could be used for productive purposes, that is, to teach people how to write better prose. Importantly, scholars selected many of the stylistic traditions with which they were familiar and introduced them to the classroom for pedagogical purposes. This focused selection of stylistic traditions and practices may have led to Winterowd's selection of the term "pedagogical stylistics" (1975, 253) to describe the pedagogies of style most common at the time. The term itself, though never widely adopted in the field, is a useful way to think about the pedagogical practices that became commonplace in composition classrooms at that time, many of them grounded in linguistics. Beyond the conscious selection of stylistic practices, the belief that theory could be used to generate language characterized a variety of works on style both inside and outside the field. Some works that influenced composition include Martin Joos's *The Five Clocks* (1962) and two books by Walker Gibson, *Tough, Sweet and Stuffy* (1966) and *Persona: A Style Study for Readers and Writers* (1969).

While interdisciplinary work from individual scholars like Joos and Gibson clearly informed the work on style during this period, most of the published work hailed from edited collections in composition and the broader field of English studies. Some of the collections published during the time period included, for example, Martin Steinmann's *New Rhetorics* (1967) and Glen Love and Michael Payne's *Contemporary Essays on Style* (1969). In 1970, Young, Becker, and Pike published their groundbreaking book on tagmemic rhetoric, *Rhetoric: Discovery and Change*. Other works in the field included Lanham's *Style: An Anti-Textbook* (1974); Winterowd's *Contemporary Rhetoric* (1975); Donald Daiker, Andrew Kerek, and Max Morenberg's *Sentence Combining and the Teaching of Writing* (1979); and Donald McQuade's *Linguistics, Stylistics, and the Teaching of Composition* (1979). These works were joined in the early 1980s by such single-authored books as Lanham's *Literacy and the Survival of Humanism* (1983b) and Patrick Hartwell's *Open to Language* (1982), a textbook that focused on the use of style in composition pedagogy.

Given the fact that Tate's first *Teaching Composition* collection (1976) represented a snapshot of the interests within composition studies at that time, it is significant that just 11 years later, he published a revised and enlarged edition, *Teaching Composition: Twelve Bibliographic Essays* (1987), with a far different emphasis. For example, Winterowd's contribution to the second edition, "Literacy, Linguistics, and Rhetoric" (1987), was a significant revision of—and departure from—his earlier article "Linguistics and Composition" (1976). As the new title alone intimates, a dramatic change in the influence of language theories on composition had occurred in the intervening years, and part of that shift involved the vastly diminishing influence of pure linguistics on the field. In the revised article, which might be characterized as "post-Golden Age" in that it appeared in 1987, it is important to note that Winterowd called linguistics "a branch of rhetoric" (265) that is "meaningless outside the context of literacy" (266), and his discussion of the linguistic influences on style comprised just a small part of a broader discussion about the developing influence of new social theories of language. In just 11 years, the world of composition had undergone a significant transformation. Indeed, Winterowd's changed emphasis was critical as a barometer of far broader shifts within the field of composition, including the adoption of many new perspectives on language.

During this period of change, composition drew increasingly upon theories from a number of new areas, despite retaining some overall affiliation with the discipline of linguistics. However, it is clear that composition's consistent movement away from formal linguistics has been concurrent with the development of various language theories, such as literacy, social and public theories of writing, postmodernism and poststructural approaches to literature and composition, and new theories of rhetoric. At the same time, the discipline of linguistics itself changed during this time period, adopting a quantitative and formal focus that arguably put it outside the practical use of scholars in various areas of composition and English studies (see Crowley 1989). Additionally, as a field composition became disillusioned with the idea that language can *explain* meaning, and that idea led the field to seek other, largely social and rhetorical, approaches to writing. Thus, even though one aim of stylistic study is to analyze language features restricted to certain social contexts and to classify those features based upon a view of their function in those contexts (the field of sociolinguistics specifically took up this charge), composition's movement away from linguistics, though gradual, proved inexorable.

As the change in the first and second versions of Winterowd's article suggests convincingly, then, the tide had shifted in the years separating their publication. While interest in the study of style grew exponentially during the three-decade Golden Age of style, Connors (2000) has shown that attention to style studies dropped off abruptly in about 1985 or 1986—the end of the Golden Age. Despite the sea change in the influence of various theories and disciplines on composition during that time, it is still difficult to ascertain what happened specifically to the study of style. Why did the field abandon style? Did composition's turn to more social, political, and public views of language and more rhetorical approaches to teaching and theorizing about writing lead to the neglect of style? Did the disappearance of stylistic interest in composition occur in part because of the *mistaken* tendency to associate the canon of style with current-traditional rhetoric instead of the process-oriented approaches to writing that had begun to dominate the field? Given what appears to be the sudden demise of the study of style, what has caused a recent resurgence of interest in the topic as well as calls for further study? Why is the time ripe *now* to reevaluate the function and uses of style in composition theory and practice?

While most critics would agree that the field, in the aftermath of a "social turn" and "public turn" (see Mathieu 2005)[2] in composition, has "moved on" from some of the linguistic-based practices once at the heart of the study of style, I contend that a broad range of stylistic practices, though once linguistically based, are consonant with composition's socially based approaches and complement the field's diverse interests in a number of rhetorical areas. One example of this is Bruce McComiskey's use of critical discourse analysis in *Teaching Composition as a Social Process* (2000). In addition, evidence of the continuing importance of style can be found today in areas of the discipline where stylistic analysis is deployed, although almost never under the name of "style." I attempt to characterize the state of style as it exists today and to contrast that status with its use during the process era in composition studies. The study of style is also prospective, pointing forward to the ways in which it might be redeployed in composition theories and practices and in other disciplinary areas. In these contexts, I argue, the availability of a reservoir of stylistic features would offer valuable help to writers, teachers, and students at all stages of the writing process.

GOING PUBLIC WITH STYLE

It seems clear that the debate about style is currently controlled by "the public intellectual" (Farmer 2002), the common term given to those outside the field of composition who often set the parameters for discussions on various issues within the discipline, usually without composition's answering word (see Chap. 5). In general, these individuals are either cultural critics or those with a passion for language who want to preserve standards that they see as being eroded. William Safire, in his widely read column for the *New York Times Magazine*, "On Language," discusses the newspaper's "sternly prescriptive" style manual intended to discourage writers from a "pushmipullyu style" that Safire sees as deviating from civility. While acknowledging that "a stylistic rule is not a law" (1999), Safire nonetheless advocates adopting a style governed by rules of grammar and usage that give the impression that the author does not acknowledge a wealth of language variation. Like Safire, David Mulroy (2003), in his book *The War against Grammar*, argues that university professors have ignored grammar instruction in their classrooms and should improve their own knowledge of grammar and usage. Additional evidence of the public's interest in style as grammar can be found in the success of Lynne Truss's *Eats, Shoots & Leaves: The Zero Tolerance Approach to Punctuation* (2004).

While composition has ventured into many new areas significant to the field, its neglect of the study of style comes at a price. The public conceptions controlling debates on style today—which often reduce style to the equivalent of grammar or prescriptive rules—have effectively usurped the topic from the discipline itself. In the process, notions of style outside the field have paralyzed those within it. While, on the one hand, resisting reductive definitions of style—and of the field—as remedial, composition professionals have nevertheless been forced to accept these public constructions, unable to refute views to which the field itself refuses to respond. I propose, therefore, that it is time for composition to take back the discussion of style—to redefine the way the conversation is framed and, by extension, to reclaim an area of theory and practice that can be a valuable source for language users. As a field, composition must exploit the resources that stylistic study identifies and, at the same time, reanimate style on our own terms—as a group of language experts who can provide the leadership to re-educate writers and a public passionately interested in the study of style, but often unable to see beyond its prescriptive affiliations.

I contend, furthermore, that this exigency is even more urgent than it may at first appear. Unless, and until, the field of composition takes up the issue of style directly, pressures from outside the field will continue to make it difficult for the field to be heard in other vital areas of its disciplinary work. In other words, it can be argued that the study of style has forged a Maginot line around the discipline beyond which it has been unable to move. The canon of style, then, represents a space where composition is forced to operate at uncertain borders and face occasional incursions from those outside the field who seek to attack the discipline at its very roots (see Mac Donald 1995; Menand 2000; Fish 2002, 2005). Sometimes constructed as an "insignificant" area of scholarship, composition and rhetoric may be able to move beyond its sometimes devalued status in the humanities through the study of style. While scholars within the field have recently taken note of the critical state of composition as a discipline (e.g., Smit 2004), no one has explored the importance of style as a way of elevating the field to a more productive and respected position within the humanities.

The discipline of composition has an ambivalent relationship with style that has placed the topic on a dividing line both inside and outside the field. In essence, the lack of interest in style exhibited by composition has deferred conceptions of style to conventional wisdom about what constitutes "good writing." These ideas about style focus on rules of usage and shibboleths of "good style," such as Strunk and White's "clarity, sincerity, and brevity" (2000). This arena of stylistic study is particularly hard to evaluate because most of it is controlled by a group of self-declared experts in style outside the field of composition. Although a few scholars within the field (Williams 1994; Kolln 1999, 2007; Coe 1987, 1998; Lanham 1974, 1976, 1983a, b, 1993, 2006) concentrate their scholarship on style, they are generally not the ones to whom the media or others turn to analyze or comment on stylistic issues. One result of the severely limited attention to style in composition is that there is no recent central body of scholarship (with a few notable exceptions, such as Johnson and Pace's *Refiguring Prose Style* 2005) that identifies style as a concern in the field; this gap defers authority to commentators generally untrained in composition scholarship, history, and theory.

The distinction between popular and academic concerns about style is often conflated in so-called style manuals or handbooks. In the popular arena, these trace their origin to Strunk and White's *Elements of Style* (2000). Today, however, most publishers of composition texts offer their own version of handbooks, where style tends to be conflated with grammar or used reductively, as in this statement from the *Longman Writer's Companion*: "Editing means adjusting sentences and words for clarity, style, economy, and correctness" (Anson, Schwegler, and Muth 2003, 73). This sentence conflates matters of grammar and usage (including correctness) with style. The irony of such an approach is that it internalizes an external view of style within the field, at once accepting popular conceptions of the meaning of style and at the same time resisting that meaning, given the field's superior knowledge. One purpose of my book is to evaluate how one popular myth in particular—that of clarity—has controlled the discussion of and shaped the conversation about style in the field for many years. I focus the myth of clarity through the figure of the public intellectual and what I contend is an absence of discussion about style in the field. I point out the difficulty of composition's relinquishment of the debate to outsiders and suggest what it would mean to explain issues to a broad audience as composition-trained public intellectuals (see Chap. 5).

PURPOSES AND AIMS OF THIS BOOK

Given the current state of affairs in stylistic studies, what would it mean to reclaim this area of study in the field? Does composition's heritage account for style's relatively recent Golden Age that has extensive links to traditions of Greek- and Roman-based rhetoric, literary stylistics, and other influences that have approached the study of style in significant ways? I look back at this recent period to correct current impressions of how style actually functioned at that time in composition and rhetoric—to show how central it was in the field and the varied ways in which it was addressed; in particular, I reveal how style was an integral part of what we now call the process movement in composition. In essence, I recuperate the uses of style during that period and present a more accurate picture of how it was conceived of and used pedagogically and practically in the field. Specifically, I focus on the productive and inventive uses of style. Thus, mine will be a revisionist's view of that period of stylistic presence in that it will reexamine some of the labels or conceptions that have come to be associated with style studies and investigate their origin and accuracy (see Chap. 3).

In addition to its retrospective view, my book also looks prospectively at the implications of a crucial paradox for the field. Even as style appears to be invisible in composition, I contend that it is at the same time ubiquitous, having diffused into other areas of the discipline under different names and ideas. In making this argument, I borrow the framework that composition scholar Janice Lauer has established for rhetorical invention, which, she argues, has "migrated, entered, settled, and shaped many other areas of theory and practice in rhetoric and composition" (2002, 2). My goal, simply stated, is to find the same evidence of style's invisible migration in the work of our field. One of my aims, then, is to examine why style has in essence "gone underground," its diffusion a testament to its continuing, if latent, importance. If style has, as Connors and Cheryl Glenn tell us, "diffused into one of the most important canons of rhetoric" (1999, 232), then why must we look so hard to find evidence of it? I propose that the answer to the paradox is intricately connected to the claims my book makes about the field's neglect of style and its view of past stylistic practices as an unwelcome legacy. I argue that this approach is based on misunderstandings about the potential uses and functions of the canon of style in composition.

In light of what is arguably the simultaneous submergence and re-emergence of style in the field, I propose that the time is ripe to reevaluate the place of style in the discipline of composition. In *Out of Style*, therefore, I investigate the state of our current understanding of style in the field. What is missing in the way that "style" often gets taken up in the field as simply a remnant of current-traditional rhetoric or as a synonym—or pseudonym—of grammar? For years, the realm of rhetoric was reduced to the domain of style and delivery. In light of the recuperation of invention and arrangement in composition, how can we support a view of rhetoric in composition studies today that is not reduced to style, but includes it in dynamic ways? How might the field gain by elaborating a more complete view of style, with greater attention to its dynamic nature and connections to invention, the process movement, and other canons of rhetoric? What if that reanimation were invested in a broad range of study going beyond syntactic practices and incorporating a number of the areas that scholars found worthy of pursuit during the Golden Age and the process era in composition and rhetoric? As James Jasinski has asked, "What might it mean to take style seriously as a topic for theoretical reflection and critical analysis?" (2001, 537).

PROLEGOMENON TO FURTHER WORK

While *Out of Style* stands on its own as an account of the state of style in the field of composition today, it also serves as a prelude to further work that needs to be done. Thus, it can be seen as the first step in a full reintegration of the study of style into the discipline. My focus is on revisiting and correcting some of the misconceptions that have developed. The chapters set the stage for a historical reconstruction of what was studied during the Golden Age or process era, how it was used and valued, and what needs to be revalued through a careful reconsideration of work that exists in style studies, some of which is not obvious. I argue that various forces and ways of thinking have distorted our ability to think about style productively. I examine how that distortion has happened and why. With the idea of correcting misconceptions as a dominant theme, here is what each of the following chapters contributes to the book:

Chapter two examines how the history of style has set the stage for the arguments made in the book. It shows the way in which many of the issues discussed were part of Greek and Roman rhetoric, and the rupture that occurred during the Renaissance. It also sets forth relevant contemporary theories of style and stylistic traditions.

Chapter three corrects the misapprehension, largely through retrospective accounts, that style did not constitute part of the process era. It shows some of the clear links between the canons of style and invention and makes the argument that during the process era, style was considered a productive and dynamic source of language innovation.

Chapter four shows that despite the apparent invisibility of style in the field today, it is wrong to think that it is no longer a part of the field. Rather, style is often hidden, having dispersed into a "diaspora" of composition studies, where it is being used in important ways.

Chapter five examines some of the ways that myths about style have filtered into the field, often through a group of public intellectuals who present style reductively in the public sphere, as equivalent to "grammar," for instance. The chapter argues that it is time for the discipline to take back the discussion of style and reclaim it as a topic of serious scholarly inquiry as composition-trained public intellectuals.

Chapter six explains what can be done to revitalize style in composition. It points to work the field can take up, explores the implications of the work done in this book, and invites the discipline to join in a renaissance of style studies in composition.

2

HISTORICAL DEVELOPMENTS

Relevant Stylistic History and Theory

Scholars today often construct a dualistic view of style, seeing it, on the one hand, as added on to thought (the approach most often affiliated with the Sophists) or, on the other hand, as organically connected to thought through nature, purpose, logic, arrangement, and other features (the perspective attributed to Aristotle) (Kinneavy 1971, 358). While characterizing style according to this binary may make sense historically, these respective approaches tell only part of the story: I propose a more complex view in which this dialectic connotes a push-pull influence in the history of style, one that represents a constant tension between constraint and excess, conciseness and amplification (see Laib 1990, 443) and that adumbrates a fundamental debate—ultimately a rhetorical one—about the function of language in society and culture. In this chapter, tailored to my overall argument, I reread parts of the history of style as essentially a clash between opposing forces that attempt either to expand or to restrain stylistic resources. Thus, in contrast to what has come to be called, often pejoratively, the "Sophistic view" of rhetoric, which generally defines style as "mere" ornamentation with no meaning-making features, I contend that stylistic history in reality constitutes an ongoing tension among the so-called "virtues" of style—clarity, correctness, propriety, and ornamentation—the weight accorded each one, their connection to other canons of rhetoric, and their affiliation with the so-called levels of style: plain, middle, and grand. In the focused account that follows—intended not to chronicle the history of style but to trace specific historical developments related to my argument—I analyze how rhetors conceived of style through history and deployed its resources according to fundamental differences in beliefs about the appropriate function of language in culture.[1]

THE SOPHISTS AND PLATO

The Sophists, a group of ancient Greek rhetors who established schools and generally charged students fees for their services, are often affiliated with a perspective that sees stylistic elements as ornamentation, that is, as form added on to content through the use of tropes, figures (of thought and speech), and other stylistic elements, including, for example, amplification, which Nevin Laib defines as "elaboration, emphasis, and copiousness of style" (1990, 443). While a number of early Greek rhetors share that reputation, one person to whom it is almost universally attributed is Gorgias who, in a style later critiqued by Plato, employs elevated, sometimes exaggerated features, including a playful attention to rhythm, poetry, and "rhetorical figures and flourishes" (Kennedy 1999, 32). Adopting an ornamental style reprised by many who followed him, Gorgias uses deviations from standard language, unusual syntax, and tropes such as parallelism and antithesis to evoke certain emotions on the part of the audience. In his "Encomium of Helen," for example, in which he pays homage to Helen of Troy through epideictic rhetoric, Gorgias makes use of stylistic ornamentation to achieve his meaning, as is evident in his introduction to the work:

> What is becoming to a city is manpower, to a body beauty, to a soul wisdom, to an action virtue, to a speech truth, and the opposites of these are unbecoming. Man and woman and speech and deed and city and object should be honored with praise if praiseworthy and incur blame if unworthy, for it is an equal error and mistake to blame the praisable and to praise the blamable. (1972, 50)

Within the context of what is later identified by Theophrastus, a student of Aristotle, as four stylistic virtues—clarity, correctness, propriety (or appropriateness), and ornamentation (or embellishment)—it is apparent that the resources Gorgias draws upon are intended to appeal to the audience principally through ornamentation in the form of tropes and schemes. For example, in the first sentence, he inverts the normal word order (*anastrophe*), uses "for" at the beginning of successive clauses as a linking word known as *anaphora* (initial repetition), and deploys the trope of *ellipsis* (deliberate omission) by not repeating the verb "is." In the second sentence, Gorgias achieves the opposite effect through the use of antithesis, and then, in the third sentence, uses *polysyndeton,* with his repetition of the conjunction "and," thereby giving not only a climactic sense to the need for people to honor Helen but also an equality of animate and inanimate objects. Other techniques include alliteration and an ending *chiasmus* that reverses the order in a reciprocal exchange of words, all of which call attention to the stylistic elements in the work. It is clear that in his approach to style, Gorgias freely employs stylistic flourishes and celebrates the play of language through rhetorical devices related to the substance of his message. I argue that the impact is not merely ornamental—what some, for example, have deemed an overabundance of antithesis, parallelism, alliteration, and assonance. Rather, Gorgias's style is intimately bound up with other rhetorical canons like invention and delivery.

If Gorgias initiates an expectation of praise designed to revive Helen's reputation in Greek society, excusing her for the inability to resist the power of language, how does he achieve his goal stylistically? Gorgias uses style rather ingeniously to pose conditional situations that, with each level of apparent betrayal of Greek society, allow him to vindicate Helen for her ostensible infractions. In that light, his repetition of the conditional "if" clause—a figure of speech known as *epanaphora*—helps Gorgias examine each potential scenario and invent in each new circumstance a reason for Helen's exoneration: "If then one must place blame on Fate and on a god, one must free Helen from disgrace"; "but if she was raped by violence and illegally assaulted and injustly insulted"; "but if it was speech which persuaded her and deceived her heart"; for if it was love that did all these things" (Gorgias 1972, 51–52). In this sense, the very form of Gorgianic prose helps to structure the way in which Greek thought is effectively reshaped, influencing the audience to reconsider the story from Helen's point of view and, in the process, to change cultural views about the heroine.

This combination of style and other rhetorical elements is evident in other Sophistic works as well. For instance, Lysias, one of the Ten Attic Orators and a Sophist known for his plain style, introduced the practice of *ethopoeia*, a device that James Murphy describes as "the ability to capture the ideas, words, and style of delivery suited to the person for whom the address is written" (1995). Ethopoeia is designed to discover, through a combination of invention, style, and delivery, the best method of persuading an audience, or what Murphy calls "discovering the exact lines of argument that will turn the case against the opponent." For Lysias, that venue was the courtroom in which the orator used forensic rhetoric for persuasion. To be most effective, Lysias adopted a plain style suitable to his courtroom audience. As Murphy explains, "Thus, *in style and in invention of argument*, Lysias mastered the art of forensic rhetoric as it was practiced by ordinary Athenians in the courtroom of his day" (43; emphasis added). The combination of invention, style, and, indeed, delivery practiced by Lysias is evident toward the end of his speech "On the Refusal of a Pension to the Invalid" (1967), when he adopts an ethopoeic stance through the frequent use of rhetorical questions. Lysias states:

> No, no gentlemen; you must not vote that way. And why should I find you thus inclined? Because anyone has ever been brought to trial at my instance and lost his fortune? There is nobody who can prove it. Well, is it that I am a busybody, a hothead, a seeker of quarrels? That is not the sort of use I happen to make of such means of subsistence as I have. That I am grossly insolent and savage? Even he would not allege this himself, except he should wish to add one more to the series of his lies. Or that I was in power at the time of the Thirty, and oppressed a great number of citizens? (531)

Lysias's rhetorical questions anticipate those the jury itself asks and thereby invent a natural progression of substantive material the jury would arguably already have on its mind. In addition, Lysias uses *asyndeton* ("a busybody, a hothead, a seeker of quarrels?") to build dramatically, through the omission of conjunctions, to a climax and concomitantly disable the list of potentially negative appellations that could be attributed to the defendant. In this instance, of course, it is also valuable to consider the delivery of the speech, with the pause listeners hear between questions and answers signaling the way style works to produce an expectation of the substantive remarks that follow sequentially. His direct address to jury members, with his use of repetition ("no, no; that . . . that") and parallelism, are other stylistic features that add to his persuasive appeal.

Despite Lysias's inventive use of ethopoeia, scholar Gary Katula (1995) perpetuates a view of Sophistic style as mere embellishment that endures today. In his analysis of Lysias's "On the Refusal of a Pension to the Invalid," Katula, noting the absence of a significant number of tropes and figures in the speech, argues that the "use of parallel phrasing is a perfect example of style supporting substance rather than being an ornamental technique." Katula contends, in other words, that Lysias shows restraint by using "his plainest language, the speech of the marketplace" and by restricting his use of figures of speech only to parallel phrases that "dramatize the contrasts between justice and injustice, between the healthy and the infirm, between the poor and the rich" (230). Katula's point is that Lysias, with his absence of "ornamental techniques," employs a measured style appropriate for courtroom oratory. Yet, a careful analysis suggests that Katula's claim does not fully capture the inventive nature of the Lysian oration. While it is true that Lysias's style falls more toward clarity and correctness than the embellishment that Katula considers its antithesis, the overall qualities of Lysias's style—as the use of rhetorical questions indicates—go beyond mere parallelism. To cite another example, when Lysias asks his adversary about his client's potential wrongdoing ("a busybody, a hothead, a seeker of quarrels?") (Lysias 1967, 531), he uses the figure of speech known as *hypophora* (inquiring what an adversary might say against us), a figure of repetition that ironically serves to mitigate the impact of the defendant's possible infractions. Thus, even within the context of the ethopoeic courtroom, stylistic ornamentation works to evaluate, and respond to, the rhetorical situation.

One other characteristic of Sophistic style is its tendency toward periodicity, a contrast with the "loose" sentences generally used in discourse today. While the periodic sentence, which works to defer the emphasis in a sentence until the end and builds a sense of anticipation, was used in varying degrees by most of the Sophists, it was arguably Isocrates' most effective device for achieving his stylistic and rhetorical aims. Paradoxically, the periodic sentence generates stylistic and substantive tension even as it works to resolve it. As Murphy states, "Just as the repetition of similar sound patterns produces an expectancy that some break in the aural pattern will occur in order to relieve the psychological tension, the accumulation of ideas also develops an expectation that there will be a final logical resolution" (1995, 48). Hence, the idea that style presupposes a substantive emotional response on the part of the audience exists structurally within the periodic sentence. In *Against the Sophists,* for instance, Isocrates (1929) uses the periodic sentence to criticize some practices of Sophistic teachers, who claimed to teach wisdom through training in public speaking but often taught it by rote, a practice arguably motivated by profit. Isocrates attempts to make his critique of this group of Sophists more powerful by reserving his main point until the end of the sentence:

> When, therefore, the layman puts all these things together and observes that the teachers of wisdom and dispensers of happiness are themselves in great want but exact only a small fee from their students, that they are on the watch for contradictions in words but are blind to inconsistencies in deeds, and that, furthermore, they

> pretend to have knowledge of the future but are incapable either of saying anything pertinent or of giving any counsel regarding the present, and when he observes that those who follow their judgments are more consistent and more successful than those who profess to have exact knowledge, then he has, I think, good reason to contemn such studies and regard them as stuff and nonsense, and not as a true discipline of the soul. (167)

Clearly, this periodic sentence serves to heighten expectations and to add emphasis to Isocrates' critique of Sophistic teaching. What may not seem as apparent, however, is the way in which the periodic sentence serves to invent subject matter, its clauses leading the reader to Isocrates' conclusion about the limits of Sophistic rhetoric. At the same time, the periodic sentence appears to be a hybrid in terms of the Theophrastan virtues, falling somewhere between clarity and ornamentation or, put differently, between a plain and high style. What seems striking about Isocrates' use of the periodic sentence is that the list of Sophistic wrongs, enumerated one after the other in the first part of the sentence, works to defer, at each step, the listener from drawing his or her own conclusion. Put differently, what appears to be the individual sins of the Sophists, which readers are given the autonomy to accept or reject after each clause, accumulatively lead the audience to one ineluctable conclusion offered by the rhetor: that some of the Sophists have not acted disinterestedly in teaching rhetoric to Athenian students.

While the style of Gorgias, Lysias, Isocrates, and other Sophists seems geared more toward language's productive qualities than many might allow, it is important nonetheless to address the reservations Plato expressed about Sophistic rhetoric. In his writing, Plato often delineates his criticisms about style more broadly under his discussion of rhetoric, a move Jasper Neel explains in his book *Plato, Derrida, and Writing* (1988) when he writes, "*Phaedrus* implies that style and rhetoric are the same and that matter precedes and enables them" (63). Plato's critique of Sophistic rhetoric—and hence, style—is essentially that it connotes flattery and deceit, primarily, he argues, because rhetoric does not have a subject matter of its own. Like cooking or cosmetics, rhetoric, in Plato's view, is merely speech about appearances. It is based too much on probability and the changing situation, or *kairos.* Thus, Plato's critique effectively reduces Sophistic rhetoric—and concomitantly, style—to an art that, while persuasive, does not achieve the absolute truth Plato considers essential for society. Given the powerful critique Plato discusses first in *Gorgias* and then softens somewhat in *Phaedrus* (though both represent a curtailing of stylistic power), how is it possible to articulate a response to Plato's reservations based on the style of the Sophists themselves?

First, it is clear that Plato's view of what he considers the counterfeit nature of rhetoric is based in part on his objection to stylistic flourishes in the Sophists. In the dialogue *Gorgias* (1925), for example, Plato considers cookery a "habitude" rather than an art. He writes:

> This practice, as I view it, has many branches, and one of them is cookery; which appears indeed to be an art but, by my account of it, is not an art but a habitude or knack. I call rhetoric another branch of it, as also personal adornment and sophistry—four branches of it for four kinds of affairs. (313)

He goes on to assert that "the art of flattery," in the form of rhetoric, acts by "insinuating herself into each of those branches, pretends to be that into which she has crept, and cares nothing for what is the best, but dangles what is most pleasant for the moment as a bait for folly, and deceives it into thinking she is of the highest value" (318–19). In contrast to the logical forms of rhetoric and argumentation that he considers appropriate, he deems the Sophistic approach akin to a manipulative interloper. He writes, "Thus cookery assumes the form of medicine, and pretends to know what foods are best for the body" (319). It is evident, then, that his construction of sophistry and adornment as cookery anticipates a much-maligned view of style. It is, after all, the stylistic aspect of sophistry that seems to concern those who contrast the supposedly additive features of linguistic ornamentation with more substantive approaches.

As far as Plato is concerned, Neel argues, "There is nothing wrong with style, of course, just so long as it comes *after* and remains *subservient to* matter, which alone can be 'true'" (1988). In the deployment of style, then, Plato seems clearly to want to rein in what he considers its deceitful excesses because like cookery, he reasons, it has no subject matter of its own; hence, like rhetoric, it is a knack rather than a virtue. As Neel points out, however, Plato's abjuration of style is in itself a form of deceit. Neel writes, "He does not want us to notice that his maneuver depends on a style so sophisticated that it seems to be absent" (63). In the *Phaedrus*, Socrates argues about the inadequacy of the Lysian speech Phaedrus has memorized, suggesting that the arrangement is to be praised, but not the invention, which can be lauded only in speeches where the arguments "are not inevitable and are hard to discover" (Socrates 1914, 439).

In what next appears to be a critique of Lysian stylistic excess—Socrates states that Lysias has repeated the same idea two or three times throughout the speech—Socrates responds to Phaedrus's suggestion that the diction and copiousness of Lysias's speech are unparalleled:

> What? Are you and I to praise the discourse because the author has said what he ought, and not merely because all the expressions are clear and well rounded and finely turned? For if that is expected, I must grant it for your sake, since, because of my stupidity, I did not notice it. I was attending only to the rhetorical manner. (Socrates 1914, 437)

Socrates' critique suggests that style fails to encourage sophisticated arguments identified as not inevitable or as hard to discover. However, what Plato fails to consider is that Phaedrus's recitation of Lysias's speech itself provides a form of invention for Socrates to use throughout the dialogue. Thus, even those Lysian arguments that Plato labels "inevitable" lead to further invention. While Plato may consider them merely ornamental, or as part of arrangement rather than invention, these elements clearly enable further invention, which suggests that the stylistic excess Plato so vigorously critiques has an important—and substantive—role.

ARISTOTLE AND DEMETRIUS

If Plato and the Sophists represent two opposing attitudes toward style, Aristotle reflects a balance of the two, an outcome not surprising given his adherence to the concept of a "mean" between ordinary speech and poetic language. "The concept of a mean between extremes," writes George Kennedy, translator of Aristotle's *On Rhetoric*, "is a characteristic doctrine of Aristotelian ethics that finds application to rhetoric as well" (Aristotle 1991, 91). Similarly, Theophrastus, Aristotle's pupil, as D'Alton (1962) suggests, works to define "the 'Mean' in which the perfection of all good style lay" (72). Even though Aristotle, according to Kennedy, sees style as a choice of words with "a quality of distinction or unfamiliarity" (91), several factors indicate that his is a view that seeks to rein in or restrain style—essentially to find what he considered the basis of propriety. First, Aristotle associates style predominately with just three of the four "virtues" later enumerated by Theophrastus: clarity and propriety (or appropriateness), which contains the idea of correctness, but without ornamentation. Murphy explains that for Aristotle "language cannot achieve its function if it is not clear, and it will not persuade if it is not appropriate" (1995, 103). Second, for Aristotle, style is most often associated with the appropriate use of metaphor. In *Rhetoric*, Aristotle states that metaphor "gives style clearness, charm, and distinction as nothing else can" (1954, 168). What is especially notable, however, is that metaphors have the power to make meaning. Aristotle discusses the invention of metaphors and suggests that "words express ideas, and therefore those words are the most agreeable that enable us to get hold of new ideas. . . . It is from metaphor that we can best get hold of something fresh" (186).

On the one hand, then, Aristotle's attention to metaphor suggests an inventive use of language and an expansive move rhetorically. On the other hand, however, despite his recognition of metaphor as the productive basis of style, Aristotle discusses contrasting "faults" or "bad taste in language" that results from violating the principles of clarity and appropriateness in word choice, suggesting his effort to restrain style as a general principle. According to Aristotle, the faults consist of the misuse of compound words (e.g., "*many-visaged* heaven"); the use of "strange words" (e.g., Alcidamas's discussion of "the *witlessness* of nature"); inappropriate epithets (meaning "long, unseasonable or frequent"; e.g., Alcidamas's use of "the laws *that are monarchs of states*" instead of "laws"); and "inappropriate"—far-fetched or grand and theatrical—metaphors (e.g., Gorgias's "events that are green and full of sap") (Aristotle 1954, 171–73). It is clear that these "faults" indicate a way in which Aristotle essentially contains style by narrowing the notion of appropriate discourse. Aristotle's specific examples suggest his critique of more expansive techniques employed by some of the Sophists. The very name of "bad taste in language" indicates the need to control, balance, and find a mean in a manner consistent with the constant push-pull influence of style throughout history.

Aristotle's notion of faults, in fact, helps to explain his concept of appropriateness and his measured approach to style. For Aristotle, says Murphy, an appropriate style conveys the state of the writer's feelings, depicts "characters," and is proportionate to the subject matter (Murphy 1995, 102). What seems crucial at the same time, however, is that Aristotle's view of style is highly structured, constricting rather than expanding our stylistic notions, especially when the idea of bad taste in language is considered. Despite the qualities of metaphor associated with meaning-making, however, style—in Aristotle's view—does not seem to have the same inventional qualities of the Sophists. Instead, Aristotle's more reserved attribution of stylistic qualities to metaphor and a choice of words that are part of current usage suggests a practical strategy without risk, a function of style closer in some ways to Plato's, especially in Aristotle's emphasis on style as "virtue" or "excellence." Nonetheless, Aristotle's contribution is at least to some extent his theory of language that connects style with knowledge organically, despite the arguably limited sphere within which he sets the parameters of stylistic propriety. His attempt to achieve balance excludes those elements of style considered more ornamental, which he sees as excessive.

While many of the characteristics of style established by the Greeks are later taken up by the Romans and accorded levels (generally, plain, middle, and high), one unusual—and apparently unique—stylistic aspect introduced by Demetrius in his manual *On Style* (1932) is the idea of "the forceful style." Most early scholars attributed *On Style* to Demetrius of Phaleron, a Paripatetic philosopher and Athenian statesman, yet, as Kennedy (1999, 130) points out, some of the work's contents make such an attribution impossible and the confusion is probably a result of both rhetors (including the unknown Demetrius) sharing the same name. In his work *In Defence of Rhetoric,* Brian Vickers (1988) explains that the forceful style, which Demetrius discusses along with three other styles—he calls these the plain, the grand, and the elegant—is characterized in part by the use of "forceful figures" of repetition like *anadiplosis* (repetition of the last word of one clause at the beginning of the following clause), anaphora (initial repetition), and climax.

According to Doreen C. Innes (1995), "the forceful style fits the expression of strong emotion, particularly anger and invective, and the main source of examples is oratory" (331). Demetrius, whose manual appears after Aristotle's *Rhetoric* and begins with references to the latter scholar, not only considers the periodic sentence forceful, but also suggests that certain word orders are better than others. For instance, he writes that "an uninterrupted series of periods . . . is favorable to force" (Demetrius 1932, 455), especially if short. Perhaps that is why Demetrius employs figures such as asyndeton, which in its omission of conjunctions lends a sense of abruptness, to achieve emotional impact. Asyndeton is a figure also important to brevity, or conciseness, an aspect of Demetrius's forceful style that contributes to form, meaning, and emotional impact (see

Vickers 1988, 306–07). Demetrius characterizes this aspect of the style as follows: "The aim of the forcible style is to be sharp and short like the exchange of blows" (467).

CICERO AND QUINTILIAN

The same countervailing tension that exists between the Sophists and Plato and what I have labeled Aristotle's attempt to restrain Sophistic style through his idea of a "mean" also exists in Roman rhetoric in its reception of "Attic" and "Asiatic" styles. It is helpful to recall that some Roman orators or philosophers identify with Atticism, a movement that espouses simplicity in writing, often associated with the Ten Attic Orators of Greece, especially Lysias. Attic orators tend to avoid the stylistic embellishment of some of the Sophistic rhetors generally affiliated with Asiatic style. The Atticists argue that eloquence exists in pure diction and simple syntax. For his part, Roman lawyer, statesman, and orator Cicero takes issue with the Atticists and argues in a polemic against Attic style in his work, *Brutus* (1939). Yet, even though his style is often associated with the eloquence of Asiatic oratory, Cicero vigorously denies any explicit identification with that movement. At the same time, however, his style is probably closer to that of the Asiatic stylists, whose aim, according to Murphy, is "to impress and secure the attention of the audience either by fluency, by florid and copious diction and imagery, or by epigrammatic conciseness" (Murphy 1995, 158). In *Brutus*, according to G. L. Hendrickson, "From a stylistic point of view Cicero's 'orator' . . . has his roots in the copiousness, not to say grandiloquence, of the Asiatic rhetoric" (1939, 3). In line with copiousness, Cicero's style, Bizzell and Herzberg suggest, is characterized predominately by amplification, which they define in Cicero's case as "naming the same thing two or three different ways in succession, adding elaborating or qualifying clauses, and otherwise developing the periodic sentence pioneered by Isocrates" (Bizzell and Herzberg 2001, 284–85).

It goes without saying that both Attic and Asiatic styles are associated with different aspects of Sophistic rhetoric and, hence, Cicero's discussion of both perpetuates the very push-pull force between playfulness and constraint, ornamentation and clarity/correctness that I have identified. Indeed, it is true that in *Brutus* Cicero sets up a debate in which the Attic orators write elegant but lifeless and restrained prose in contrast to what one orator, Calidius, suggests is necessary to move the listener: "a more elevated style and a more vehement delivery [that] was frenzy and delirium" (Cicero 1939, 239). On the other hand, Brutus attributes to Calvus, associated with Atticism, "a meagerness of style" (247). Yet Cicero's critique of Attic style is not without its own complications. Cicero, who was accused by some of degrading Attic style, carefully sets forth the limits of his criticism:

> But if meagreness and dryness and general poverty is put down as Attic, with of course the proviso that it must have finish and urbanity and precision, that is good so far as it goes. But because there are in the category of Attic other qualities better than these, one must beware not to overlook the gradations and dissimilarities, the force and variety of Attic orators. (1939, 247)

Cicero obviously believes that the use of Attic style limits the resources available to speakers. However, he maintains a somewhat neutral position, possibly because he does not identify exclusively with either Attic or Asiatic style, but draws from both in his own style. In this regard, Richard Leo Enos, in "The Art of Rhetoric at Rhodes: An Eastern Rival to the Athenian Representation of Classical Rhetoric" (2004), which carefully documents the island's influence on Roman rhetors, including Cicero, suggests that "the more moderate alternative to the Asiatic rhetoric was the Rhodian style" (192). Enos explains that the Rhodian model—influential for Cicero, for instance, who was exposed to the rhetoric while Rhodes was under Roman rule—was known as a "moderate, balanced style of rhetoric" that stood in contrast to Asianism, which Roman Atticists, according to Enos, "considered to be excessively bombastic" (192–93). Enos suggests that this cross-cultural model, which Romans like

Cicero and Quintilian found "compatible with their open and diverse temperament," was "ideal for the study and practice of declamation" (194), widely adopted by Cicero and Quintilian and other Roman rhetors in their schools of rhetoric in Rome.

It is useful to remember, as well, that Cicero is often credited with developing the idea of the three levels of style—plain, middle, and grand—a classification scheme that first appears in the anonymous *Rhetorica ad Herennium* (1954). For Cicero, these styles are directly related to their ostensible purposes: to instruct, to delight, and to move to belief or action. In tracing the Ciceronian origins of these stylistic levels, S. Michael Halloran and Merrill D. Whitburn (1982) clarify the features of plain style, some of which overlap with middle and grand styles:

> All three styles use ornamental devices whose description and cataloging make up so much of later rhetorical theory, but in the plain style the ornamentation is supposed to be less apparent. Elaborate prose rhythm is avoided altogether, and syntax is loose rather than periodic. Only those figures of speech that would not seem radically out of place in everyday discourse are used; metaphor is particularly recommended, since it occurs quite naturally in ordinary speech. (60–61)

Halloran and Whitburn thus eschew an affiliation of levels of style with distinct genres—for example, they complicate the assumption that "plain" style is "scientific" style—and propose instead that "plain, middle, and grand styles are levels of embellishment and emotional concentration rather than generically distinct modes of language" (61). Indeed, in an approach that is suggestive of an Aristotelian movement toward a mean, Halloran and Whitburn say they consider "Cicero's view of the three styles as *symphonic*" (61; emphasis added). Thus, rather than acceding to a common tendency to make the levels distinct, they suggest that Cicero "saw these three rhetorical functions, and hence the three styles, as aspects or phases of the single process of communication by which one human intelligence influences another" (61–62).

In keeping with a balanced view of stylistic resources, Cicero also endorses, in his *Orator* (1939), a kind of prose style that varies according to the rhetorical situation. Like Lysias and his concept of ethopoeia, Cicero suggests that the contemporary usage of Roman orators should dictate their style on various occasions (see Murphy 1995, 196). Cicero makes his comments regarding the "practical value" of style in a defense against charges that his style includes excessive rhythm, ornament, and emotional emphasis in contrast to Atticism's emphasis on the logical use of language, which is closer to an Aristotelian perspective:

> As a matter of fact, the art of delivering a beautiful oration in an effective oratorical style is nothing else, Brutus . . . than presenting the best thoughts in the choicest language. Furthermore, there is no thought which can bring credit to an orator unless it is fitly and perfectly expressed, nor is any brilliance of style revealed unless the words are carefully arranged. And both thought and diction are embellished by rhythm. (Cicero 1939, 499)

In addition to *Brutus* and *Orator*, Cicero's *de Oratore* (1959) shows the connection that style shares with arrangement and invention. In a theoretical discussion of style in which he uses the character of Crassus to explain his views, Cicero writes, "Good speakers bring, as their peculiar possession, a style that is harmonious, graceful, and marked by a certain artistry and polish. Yet this style, if the underlying subject-matter be not comprehended and mastered by the speaker, but inevitably be of no account or even become the sport of universal derision" (1:39). He later reinforces the equal importance of style and content when he writes that the traits of ornateness and appropriateness mean that style "must be in the highest degree pleasing and calculated to find its way to the attention of the audience, and that it must have the fullest possible supply of facts" (3:73). In going on to describe what constitutes the stronger form of invention with respect to humor, Cicero states that it emerges from a combination of form (words) and content (fact): "A witty saying has its point sometimes in fact, sometimes in words, though people are most particularly amused whenever laughter is excited by the union of the two" (2:383). Cicero acknowledges here the contrapuntal effect of both substance and style, seeing both as essential to produce humor. Thus, a natural connection in this case exists among style, invention, and arrangement. His collective writing suggests that the study of style is intricately connected to other rhetorical canons and is far from an isolated occurrence.

If Aristotle mediates the stylistic ideas of Plato and the Sophists, the Roman orator and teacher Quintilian, an adherent of Ciceronian rhetoric, may well be seen as a kind of equal counterpart, one who arguably tips the balance toward a more restrained attitude toward style. In an approach reminiscent of Aristotle, Quintilian views the most important stylistic virtue as "perspicuity," or clarity, which has been seen at various times historically as the chief virtue to emulate. A teacher whose emphasis on style cannot be seen outside his vision of the ideal orator as "the good man speaking well," Quintilian employs a stylistic pedagogy that relies heavily on imitation and on such techniques as the *progymnasmata*, a set of graded exercises taught in school. After stating that "'embellishment' (the use of 'ornaments') is what most distinguishes each individual orator's style," Quintilian adds that "amplification, sentential epigrams, and tropes such as metaphor, allegory, and irony *should all be used but sparingly*" (Bizzell and Herzberg 2001, 296; emphasis added). In other words, Quintilian seems to propose in his stylistic virtues the same moderation he seeks to impart among personal virtues embodied in his classic saying of "the good man speaking well."

For Quintilian, then, ornament in language is important, but needs to be measured. In Book VIII of the *Institutio Oratoria*, for example, Quintilian (1953) writes, "The ornate . . . consists firstly in forming a clear conception of what we wish to say, secondly in giving this adequate expression, and thirdly in lending it additional brilliance, a process which may correctly be termed embellishment" (3:245). Insofar as his identifying clarity as the most important quality of ornamentation, Quintilian, as Bizzell and Herzberg suggest, "held up [Cicero] as a stylistic model against the elaborate ornamentation then fashionable" (Bizzell and Herzberg 2001, 39). Indeed, Quintilian himself cites Cicero for this proposition when he writes, "An acceptable style is defined by Cicero as one which is not over-elegant: not that our style does not require elegance and polish, which are essential parts of ornament, but that excess is always a vice" (3:235). Quintilian also intimates the need for balance in levels of style. He suggests that "style need not always dwell on the heights: at times it is desirable that it should sink. For there are occasions when the very meanness of the words employed adds force to what we say" (3:223). In keeping with his theory of style, Quintilian also talks about the importance of amplification without seeing it as a feature of ornamentation. He writes: "The real power of oratory lies in enhancing or attenuating the force of words. . . . The first method of amplification or attenuation is to be found in the actual word employed to describe a thing" (3:261–63). He adds that "there are four principal methods of amplification: augmentation, comparison, reasoning and accumulation" (3:265). For Quintilian, the method of amplifying material is principally through *copia*, defined as how one achieves "abundance" through the use of stylistic resources: "There can then be no doubt that he must accumulate a certain store of resources, to be employed whenever they may be required. The resources of which I speak consist in a copious supply of words and matter" (4:5).

Part of Quintilian's complete educational program for training orators involved two aspects of style: imitation, which includes reading aloud, analysis, memorization and paraphrase of models, and transliteration, among other things; and the ancient process of *progymnasmata*, essentially a group of graded composition exercises designed to develop proficiency by presentation in order of increasing difficulty. A few examples of these exercises include retelling a fable; *chreia*, or amplification of a moral theme; commonplace, or confirmation of a thing admitted; description; thesis; and laws, or arguments for or against a law (Murphy 1995, 183). One crucial aspect of Quintilian's use of imitation and *progymnasmata* to train Roman boys is improving both their inventive and stylistic abilities, a goal that continued through practice speeches known as declamation. It is clear from his emphasis on the entire educational process and the sequence of exercises combining invention with imitation that Quintilian generally saw style and invention as part of an organic process designed to train Roman orators beginning when they were young.

ERASMUS AND RAMUS

Erasmus is best known for his work *On Copia*, a compilation of two books in which he tried to help writers attain abundance of words and ideas. In his attempt to develop good style, Erasmus opposed strict adherence to Ciceronian prose, which he felt resulted in an artificial style. As Bizzell and Herzberg point out, Erasmus's emphasis on the rhetorical situation led him to adopt *copia* in its classical sense of "any abundantly varied flow of speech that impresses with its energy and inventiveness and wrings assent from the audience" (Bizzell and Herzberg 2001, 583). In developing *copia*, Erasmus cites Quintilian as an example and suggests that words and ideas (style and content) are "so interconnected in reality that one cannot easily separate one from the other" (1978). He gives the following examples of the two:

> Richness of expression involves synonyms, heterosis or enallage, metaphor, variation in word form, equivalence, and other similar methods of diversifying diction. Richness of subject matter involves the assembling, explaining, and amplifying of arguments by the use of examples, comparisons, similarities, dissimilarities, opposites, and other like procedures. (Erasmus 1978)

Erasmus was especially well known for his discussion of amplification and the exercises he designed to train others. As Edward P. J. Corbett (1971) explains, Erasmus "set the pattern for the English grammar-school curriculum and for rhetorical training in the schools." *De Copia*, widely used in the schools, was "designed to assist grammar-school students in acquiring elegance and variety of expression in Latin composition" (605). For example, Erasmus wrote 150 different ways of expressing the same sentiment, "Your letter pleased me very much." Thus, it seems that Erasmus, particularly in his emphasis on *copia* and amplification, helps expand the notion of style during the Renaissance, connecting style closely to invention through his emphasis on an abundance of words and ideas.

If Erasmus was affiliated with an expansive move on the part of rhetoric during the Renaissance, a huge change took place during the sixteenth century that affected the nature of rhetoric and style significantly and ushered in what Chaïm Perelman (1979), in *The New Rhetoric and the Humanities*, suggests is a stylistic tradition of modern rhetoric (3). In using this phrase, Perelman means the connection of rhetoric to style in a way that led to rhetoric's disrepute. Perelman focuses on the change from classical rhetoric, which included invention, arrangement, style, memory, and delivery, and its reduction to the so-called "flowers of rhetoric" (1), the canons of style and delivery only, under the influence of sixteenth-century philosopher Peter Ramus. As Perelman states, "The extraordinary influence of Ramus hindered, and to a large extent actually destroyed, the tradition of ancient rhetoric that had been developed over the course of twenty centuries and with which are associated the names of such writers as Aristotle, Cicero, Quintilian, and St. Augustine" (2). Perelman explains that Ramus separated invention and arrangement from Aristotle's conception of rhetoric and placed them instead under his newly formulated idea of dialectic. Thus, for Ramus, rhetoric included style and delivery *only* and became defined as the "art of speaking well," of "eloquent and ornate language," which included the study of tropes and of figures of style and oratorical delivery—all less important than Ramus's new philosophical dialectic. Along with this change, Perelman says, came the birth of the tradition of modern rhetoric, "better called stylistic, as the study of techniques of unusual expression" (3).

In his work *Arguments in Rhetoric against Quintilian*, Ramus (1986) sets forth his ideas of style, which Bizzell and Herzberg suggest, "seems to be a kind of applied psychology, a study of the way to frame sentences so as to force certain reactions from recalcitrant, mentally inferior audiences" (2001, 678). Under Ramistic style, tropes are reduced to metonymy, irony, metaphor, and synecdoche, but he suggested that a plain style is best. Thus, overall, it seems that his conception of style, especially in its separation from invention and arrangement and in its restricted capacity, was very much intended to restrain the nature of a stylistic rhetoric and to suggest its inferior qualities. If we accept Perelman's analysis, this new conception of rhetoric as divorced from philosophy—and excluding invention and arrangement—might be considered the beginning of what eventually led to the disappearance of style from composition. If, as Perelman suggests, "rhetoric, on this conception, is essentially an art of expression and more especially, of literary conventionalized expression; it is an art of style" (3), then the view of rhetoric as simply ornate form runs contrary to other, more contemporary theories of style.

TWENTIETH-CENTURY THEORIES OF STYLE

Of the many debates that have informed the study of style in composition studies, few have drawn more notice than that of the proper relationship between form (style) and content (meaning). As Robert Connors and Cheryl Glenn remark, "Perhaps the central theoretical problem presented by the study of style is the question of whether style as an entity really exists" (1999, 232). An affirmative response to that question emerges when style is defined as "choices of verbal formulation" (Ohmann 1967), which implies a view of style in part as preverbal thought. As Richard Ohmann suggests, the idea of style as choice applies when "another writer would have said *it* another *way*" (137). The definition of style as choice is implicit in the theory of style as "ornate form," which assumes that form is separate from content and that "ideas exist wordlessly and can be dressed in a variety of outfits depending on the need or the occasion" (Milic 1965, 67). The theory of ornate form assumes that style can be separated from meaning. In composition, this approach has been important to the belief that stylistic practices can be broken down and taught to student writers. As Ohmann writes, "The idea of style implies that words on a page might have been different, or differently arranged, without a corresponding difference in substance" (1967, 137). This "dualistic" view has been predominant in most approaches to style from both classical rhetoric and literary stylistics.

In contrast to the dualistic view of style as choice, the position that style (or form) is inseparable from content (or meaning) is known as "Crocean aesthetic monism" (Milic 1965). According to this "organic" view of style, even the slightest change in form implies a different meaning. With no seam between form and content, then, some argue that ultimately there is no such thing as "style." Stated differently, if even a simple change in form suggests a different meaning, then the logical extension of this is that "there is no style at all, only meaning or intuition" (Milic 1965, 67). While the organic theory has been considered persuasive by some composition scholars (e.g., Winterowd 1975), it has been part of an ongoing debate for years. As Roland Barthes pointed out during a symposium on literary style, the debate between the respective role of content and form goes back to Plato:

> The oldest [issue in style] is that of Content and Form. As everyone knows, this dichotomy derives from the opposition in classical rhetoric between Res and Verba: Res or the demonstrative materials of the discourse depends on Invention, or research into what one can say about a subject; on Verba depends Elocutio (or the transformation of these materials into a verbal form). This Elocutio is, roughly, our "style." (1971, 3)

Barthes goes on to explain that the relationship between form and content "is taken to be the 'appearance' or 'dress' of Content, which is the 'reality' or 'substance' of Form" (3–4).

This is what has led, says Barthes, to a situation in which "the metaphors applied to Form (style) are thus decorative: Figures, colors, nuances" (4). While ultimately most feel that form is subsumed by content, Barthes reaches the opposite conclusion in his essay, suggesting that the dichotomy, though inappropriate in the first place, should be resolved in favor of form rather than content. He writes, "We can no longer see a text as a binary structure of Content and Form; the text is not double but multiple; within it there are only forms, or more exactly, the text in its entirety is only a multiplicity of forms without a content" (6).

Another theory of style, which Louis Milic calls "individualist" or "psychological monism," is often summed up as "Style is the man." Because style is regarded as the unique expression of someone's personality, this view posits that no two writers, each having different life experiences, can express themselves in the same verbal style. As Milic states, this individualist theory ("write naturally"), which he sees as one of the predominant views of style, "has become so well established in this century that it has achieved the status of an unconscious (or unspoken) assumption and as a result is no longer stated in axiomatic form" (1975, 277). The individualist or monistic theory is in line with the definition of style as the deviation from a "norm," which implies a standardized use of language that writers have decided purposefully to deviate from in arriving at a personal style. However, as Nils Enkvist points out, some features that are labeled stylistic are not exclusive to an individual but are shared by groups (1964). Furthermore, Enkvist suggests that an added difficulty is that "to get at style, the investigator must begin with the laborious task of setting up a corpus of reference to find the norm or norms from which a given text differs" (22), which in fact some scholars have done. Clearly, the definition of style as deviation from a norm can be problematic today because, even though there is no such thing as language use without norms, there is often no common agreement—especially in the absence of a grammar of style—of what constitutes those norms and what value we should attach to them. The "Students' Right to Their Own Language" resolution illustrates the importance of this concern.

One other theoretical question about style that has had widespread implications in composition and rhetoric is whether style can be extended by analogy to include the canon of arrangement. For many years, that question has been debated as scholars in different disciplines considered the application of stylistic study to larger aspects of discourse. In composition, many scholars tried to apply stylistic principles to the paragraph, which in turn led them to examine larger discourse structures. In his contribution to a symposium on style, Enkvist proposed a compromise between the sentence itself as a "style carrier" and features that link sentences together, called "discoursal intersentence phenomena": "A large number of stylistic features are ultimately describable in terms of sentences and the comparison of sentences, but many intersentence devices may also possess stylistic relevance and should be described as such at once" (1971, 57).

While some recent writing about style in the discipline of composition has treated style as equivalent with arrangement (see Ostrom 1997), some scholars consider it useful pedagogically to maintain a distinction between the canons. This distinction corresponds to the usual way people understand style (relying on patterns of *language* use) as different from the organization (or patterns) of *ideas* in text. Thus, for example, a recent work, *Elements of Alternate Style* (Bishop 1997), attempts to extend style to the canon of arrangement, based on Winston Weathers's decision to redefine "style" to include broader forms of discourse. In *An Alternate Style: Options in Composition,* Weathers (1980) writes, "We must identify options in all areas of vocabulary, usage, sentence forms, dictional levels, paragraph types, ways of organizing material into whole compositions: options in all that we mean by style" (5). Weathers's work introduces a number of language features (e.g., "crots" and "grots") which, although named in unusual ways, are similar to certain traditional stylistic tools, such as tropes and figures. The real issue with Weathers's approach, however, is his description of style as a feature of discourse larger than the sentence, a view that includes paragraphs and essay organization, phenomena generally included under the rhetorical canon of arrangement.

The attribution of aspects of form or arrangement to style becomes a key question in *Elements of Alternate Style* (Bishop 1997). In essays like Lad Tobin's "The Case for Double-Voiced Discourse," the authors make a case for incorporating the larger features in essays. For example, Tobin's call for essays that are "multidimensional" and "multivoiced" (47) suggests descriptions of features that may apply to style on some levels, but clearly move into broader questions of form and discourse. Similarly, in "Grammar J, As in Jazzing Around," Hans Ostrom (1997), in effect, redefines style in a section entitled "Let's say style is arrangement." In his creation of the word "plerk" to describe a neologism between play and work, Ostrom exhibits the kind of "play" Richard Lanham calls for in his work on style during the 1970s and 1980s; yet Ostrom, like the other contributors, enacts style at a broader level of discourse. In this book, I argue that by looking at expositions of alternate style, the field can examine how some of these areas do impact "style"; however, it is also important to clarify the demarcation between style and broader forms of discourse. In achieving this objective, I follow the model of Tzvetan Todorov, who insists that style is separate from larger discourse structure but inextricably linked to it. In suggesting that a feature of style is relevant when related to a larger element in the text—in this case a thematic motif—Todorov argues that "thematics and stylistics confirm each other, each being at once *signifiant* and *signifié* of the other; it is here that research into coherence finds its legitimate task" (1971, 37).

The fact that these definitions and broader theories of style continue to inform the discussion of style has several implications. The question of whether there is an important split between form and content still matters to the discipline in at least one important way. Accepting for the moment my claim that style has diffused into other areas of the discipline, the question of whether the form of a person's dialect or home language can be separated from the content—here, interpreted as the person's identity—continues to trouble composition as a discipline. While this discussion will take place in Chapter five, for the moment it is enough to note that these definitions signal broad debates about the meaning of style that have an impact on the current state of style in composition studies. Because stylistics, whether based in literature, linguistics, or rhetoric and composition, has treated these theories as an important issue, it is crucial to examine how scholars are still asking the same question, even implicitly, in composition. Is it possible that no one has realized that some of these theories might be critiqued by other recent ideas in the field or that current areas of study in the field might provide a possible resolution? The possibilities for rethinking the problem of style appear throughout this book.

STYLISTIC TRADITIONS AND INFLUENCES

The following traditions of stylistic inquiry in composition will help to situate my book, and each one is important in a different way. For example, I draw on classical rhetoric and literary stylistics when I link style to invention and argue that the tacit diffusion of style into other areas of composition has prevented us from exploiting many aspects of a rich stylistic tradition. As these traditions appear in different chapters, I also draw on influences from several different contexts. These traditions are not separated by any rigid line, but rather are intricately connected to the state of style in the discipline of composition studies today.

Classical Rhetoric

The renewed interest in classical rhetoric as a force in composition studies has influenced the field's view toward style, and the central figure in that renaissance is Edward P. J. Corbett, whose writing on style nearly forty years ago still resonates today. Yet, we cannot adequately appreciate the importance of Corbett's work without citing the classical, predominantly Aristotelian, tradition in which it is situated, even though subsequently composition scholars have turned to other strands of rhetoric as well. On the basis of Aristotle's *Rhetoric*, a benchmark for Corbett, the lines are drawn to delineate style as one canon of rhetoric within a group of canons that also includes invention, arrangement, memory, and delivery. Corbett argues that the canons, despite the overlap between them, are intended to be separate, as Aristotle and Roman orators like Cicero and Quintilian made clear. Even though classical rhetoric was revived as a part of the "New Rhetoric" in the 1960s and 1970s, however, the influence of the tradition on style has had an uneven history. Many scholars like Connors and Glenn (1999) and Sharon Crowley and Debra Hawhee (2004) follow his application of the classical theories and pedagogies of style, though the division of the canons is often seen as more fluid in scholarship today.

Some composition scholars have questioned the premises of not only Corbett but others in composition who have followed his example, like Milic and W. Ross Winterowd. For example, Lanham, also drawing from classical rhetoric, challenges the idea of a clear or transparent style as the style that everyone should seek to emulate. In particular, Lanham opposes what he calls the "Clarity-Brevity-Sincerity" or "C-B-S theory of language," which he sees as the dominant view in the field of composition. Lanham contends that the C-B-S style, in which "language remains ideally passive and transparent" (1983b, 122), has the effect of urging writers to look *through* words to an underlying reality, a contention he argues should be reversed. Lanham proposes instead that we adopt an opaque style in which we look *at* the words themselves, characterized by reordering, exaggeration, repetition, discontinuity, and a return to "play." Lanham (1983b) sets forth his ideas in *Literacy and the Survival of Humanism*, where he offers a "stylistic matrix" based on the uses of what he calls "a self-conscious rhetoric . . . which in many *particular* cases energizes the greatest, and the most greatly disputed, Renaissance literary texts" (58). Lanham describes his philosophy as follows:

> I am going to call such self-conscious rhetoric, in a generic singular, the Opaque Style. What we must first notice about the Opaque Style is that it works like a simple At/Through switch. Verbal patterns can vary in small increments, but our attention does not seem to. Either we notice an opaque style as a style, (i.e., we look at it) or we do not (i.e., we look through it to a fictive reality beyond). (1983b, 58)

While also drawing upon classical rhetoric and enumerating tropes and schemes, Lanham argues against their use to produce the kind of scientific, normative prose that he sees at the heart of composition studies. In evaluating the use of classical rhetoric to discuss style in the field, then, this book explores both the continuing usefulness of its theories and pedagogies as well as some of the ways it has served to perpetuate a certain view of style in the field.

Another important aspect of classical rhetoric's clear division of canons is that invention was considered at the time as being about ideas, while style was seen as a function of language. This ends up being important in the division between the two today and the varied esteem with which each is held. Invention was the system or method for discovering ideas or arguments, a "systematized way of turning up or generating ideas on some subject" (Corbett 1971, 36). Style, on the other hand, was about language, as in Cardinal Newman's definition: "Style is a thinking out into language" (Corbett 1971, 37). While each is a separate canon of rhetoric, invention and style had important, yet often unrecognized, connections during the process era of composition studies (see Chap. 3).

Literary Stylistics

The tradition of literary stylistics is central to the way in which the study of style developed in composition studies. Drawing upon different traditions of grammar and the deployment of various levels of language such as morphological (including syntax), phonological (sound and rhythm), lexical, semantic, and so forth, the discipline of literary stylistics, which attempted to categorize and analyze both the poetry and literary prose of writers from different time periods, traditions, and languages, had a profound effect on the discipline of composition. Even a cursory examination of the interests of literary stylistics reveals the depth of that interest. In two separate conferences at Indiana University, for example, the importance of style as a multidisciplinary area of study became important. Thus, in 1960, the results of the first conference, held in 1958, were published under the title *Style in Language.* In 1971, the results of the second Indiana symposium, held in 1969, were published under the title *Literary Style: A Symposium.* In 1970, Donald Freeman published an edited collection, *Linguistics and Literary Style,* that featured articles by literary scholars under headings such as "Linguistic Stylistics: Theory and Method," "Approaches to Prose Style," and "Approaches to Metrics." Beyond the methods of analysis themselves, a key ingredient of this tradition, as taken up in composition, is the belief that style is not restricted to poetry or literature but falls within the range of general language variation, a finding supported in large part by Roman Jakobson (1960) and later affirmed by Mary Louise Pratt (1977) in *Toward a Speech Act Theory of Literary Discourse.* As Todorov states succinctly, "There is no point in separating a 'literary stylistics' from a 'linguistics stylistics': one is only the application of the other" (1971, 37).

Ideas of Plain Style

I contend that much of our discussion of style today stems from beliefs about "plain style" that have become part of our popular culture. Calling plain style "a contemporary form of the commonplace," cultural historian Kenneth Cmiel writes, "The impulse for simple, declarative sentences is strong in twentieth-century culture" (1990, 260). Cmiel points out that the plain style, along with the informal "colloquial" style and the "professional" style, were designed with a large and diverse public in mind. He contends, however, that all these styles serve to "corrode civic discussion" and that the decision to promote these ideals in culture at the beginning of the twentieth century marked a major shift. "The sanctioning of these styles in elite culture at the turn of the century is worth note, for the need to reconstruct a spirited public was a central concern of progressive social thought" (261). The way that "plain style" became accessible to all is through its notion of a transparent correctness. If style is transparent, then the only thing left to be concerned about is correctness, which everyone ostensibly can master. This idea means that the plain style is for everyone—not just the elite. Cmiel suggests, however, that certain aspects of the plain style are also problematic:

> The idiom has its virtues. It is clear and informative. It treats its audience with respect. Unlike the colloquial [style], it is supposed to contribute to discussion and not evoke feeling. Yet the plain style also has drawbacks. There is an unhealthy preoccupation with like/as distinctions or avoiding split infinitives. What is "correct" is studied at the expense of what is appropriate to the setting. The plain style also creates the illusion that language can be like a glass, a medium without the infusion of a self. It pretends the facts can speak for themselves in ways that the old rhetoric never did. The very style has helped perpetuate the belief that there are technical, apolitical solutions to political problems. It is perhaps the most deceptive style of them all. (260)

According to Cmiel, then, plain style, functioning much as a conventional belief, perpetuates certain ideas that become ingrained in the popular consciousness. I contend that writing in America today has been controlled in large part by this mythology of a plain style and that it has dictated our conceptions of what constitutes "good writing." The power that this belief exerts is one reason why it is important to question the reasoning that supports it and to determine to what extent this view has influenced the relegation of style studies to a low status in the field of composition. While the virtues of plain style seem generally accepted in composition (see, however, Lanham, for a contradictory view of this assertion), my contention is that the idea should be reexamined in both composition and ideas about writing in popular culture, especially those espoused by public intellectuals.

3

OUT OF STYLE

Reclaiming an "Inventional Style" in Composition

When scholars of recent composition history consider style, they often regard it as part of "current-traditional rhetoric," which is associated with an emphasis on the formal written product, prescriptive rules, and static language practices. Typical of such a mainstream view, Richard Young makes this arguably negative connection explicit when he states that one of the salient features of current-traditional rhetoric is its "strong concern with *usage* (syntax, spelling, punctuation) and with *style* (economy, clarity, emphasis)" (Young 1978, 31; emphasis added). Indeed, Young and his generation of scholars often place current-traditional rhetoric's emphasis on the textual product in opposition with what they identify as "the process approach," which emphasizes writing as shaped recursively through a number of cognitive, social, and cultural processes. They further delineate the process movement by associating it with the rhetorical canon of invention, defined as the discovery of ideas or of "the subject matter of discourse" (Young 1976, 1).

What these scholars have ignored, however, is the way the study of style experienced a "renaissance" (Pace 2005, 28)[1] during the same three-decade period—from the 1960s through the mid-1980s—usually considered composition's process movement and generally known today for its championing of invention. As a result of these characterizations, style now often ends up getting discussed *retrospectively* as distinct from more dynamic views of process and invention. This chapter seeks to correct that oversight: that is, to show how style, in contrast to the prevailing view, was actually an integral part of the process movement and how it serves—rather than opposes—an interest in invention, which Robert Connors and Cheryl Glenn describe as "the central, indispensable canon of rhetoric" (1999, 160).

REVISIONIST HISTORY

In contrast to conceptions prevalent in the field today, I argue that during the process era, the study of style constituted a meaningful part of language *production* for writers. According to this largely untold story, style is not the product-based residue of current-traditional rhetoric that many say it is retrospectively (see Young 1978; Berlin 1987; Crowley 1989), but rather is a dynamic feature of the very process movement the field considers crucial to its disciplinary identity. Despite what has developed as our current conventional wisdom, then, I contend that the process period actually constituted a Golden Age of style studies, a time when style pedagogy was one of the *innovations* in the field, linked to those inventive features of composition that signaled advances in meaning, knowledge, and language.

Indeed, this hypothesis gains additional support when one turns to recent work from composition scholars like Tom Pace, who argues that process-era work on style by Francis Christensen, Edward P. J. Corbett, and Winston Weathers is often seen erroneously today as overly simplistic, apolitical, and decontextualized, when the real aim of these scholars was to make stylistic options available to students and to increase their rhetorical awareness (Pace 2005, 8, 22; see also Walpole 1980). Similarly, in *A Rhetoric of Pleasure: Prose Style and Today's Composition Classroom,*[2] T. R. Johnson, in looking at various moments in rhetorical history, theorizes a "'renegade' tradition" based on authorial pleasure, but raises the possibility that, in an abandonment similar to that of style, "in recent decades, we have strenuously disavowed this sort of renegade terrain in order to ascend to positions of authority and privilege within the university." Johnson goes on to suggest that it may be time to reclaim that tradition, in part through "playing around, quite pleasurably, with devices and principles of prose style" (Johnson 2003, xii).

If recent work on style is beginning to point the field in a new direction, why is a revisionist history necessary at this juncture of composition's development? Given the ongoing binary division of invention as "central" and style as "reductive" or "static," it is crucial to correct this erroneous view and set the record straight. First, however, it is important to make clear that this dichotomization is nothing new, but results from what James Zebroski has referred to as the process movement's "invention agenda." In his article "The Expressivist Menace," Zebroski (1999) offers an explanation for the way in which composition histories tend to produce these very dichotomies, resulting from what he calls "the rhetoric of menace"—or the narrative of how the field "retrojects" or constructs the past in self-serving and pejorative ways, depending upon when a past era is being looked at, by whom, and for what purposes. It matters when a precise history gets written, Zebroski argues, since "a historical narrative emerges from the dialectic between present and past" (99). Zebroski attributes the relative rereading of history in part to the conflict between a "first generation" that initially constructs the profession in a certain way and a subsequent "revolt of the second generation" by emerging scholars whose different needs compel it to challenge the interpretation of the first generation. He explains that "retrojection of mythic histories onto the past occurs, as professionals, trying to establish themselves and their authority in the field, argue against what they take to be the essential character of first generation thought and identity" (99–100).

Similarly, Louise Wetherbee Phelps theorizes that what has occurred historically in the field might be viewed in terms of the particular "path composition has taken" in contrast with other paths the discipline has not pursued. In "Paths Not Taken: Recovering History as Alternative Future," Phelps (1999) observes that "negative and positive versions of 'what happened' converge through strategies and tropes of mutual accommodation favoring the dominant position." Once a particular path is taken, Phelps asserts, it is difficult to overcome the belief that a different option the field may *at one point* have chosen is already lived through, over and done with, fixed, unchangeable, shaped through convergent choices into the single "path," "mainstream," "paradigm," or (most tellingly) into the "system." If the past converges and solidifies into the path taken, what remains today of multiple "paths not taken" becomes invisible (42).

Zebroski and Phelps help explain why composition scholars, in an attempt to resurrect the canon of invention after years of neglect, constructed it as a dynamic aspect of rhetoric in direct contrast to style, perceived to belong, on the other hand, to a static, current-traditional rhetoric. Through the process of retrojection, therefore, the same opposition that developed between "product" and "process" and "current-traditional" and "new" rhetoric (see Phelps 1988; Crowley 1989) produced, as Elizabeth Rankin stated, "a similar implied opposition between invention and style" (Rankin 1985, 9). Maxine Hairston reinforced this dichotomy in her influential article, "The Winds of Change," where she wrote that "teachers who concentrate their efforts on teaching style, organization, and correctness are not likely to recognize that their students need work in invention" (Hairston 1990, 7). James Berlin and Robert Inkster articulated the opposition even more forcefully in an article that appeared in *Freshman English News*, stating that the current-traditional paradigm "neglects invention almost entirely . . . and makes style the most important element in writing" (Berlin and Inkster 1980, 4).

THE WRONGFUL RIFT BETWEEN STYLE AND INVENTION

While claims about the respective roles of invention and style may seem part of a natural evolution in composition studies, it seems clear that the declining fortunes of style during the process movement resulted in part from the effort by some scholars to distance it from invention and to affiliate it with an increasingly derided current-traditional rhetoric. That affiliation, I assert, began in 1959, when the term "current-traditional rhetoric," once a neutral term, started to take on increasingly pejorative connotations with Daniel Fogarty's *Roots for a New Rhetoric.* In his book, Fogarty characterized current-traditional rhetoric as "still largely Aristotelian in its basic philosophy," and he included among its core elements grammar, spelling, and mechanics; the four modes of discourse; and "style qualities," which he defined as "clearness, force, coherence, interest, naturalness, and other devices" (Fogarty 1959, 118). He contrasted the stylistic features of a current-traditional rhetoric that he saw as emphasizing form over content with "a new or improved teaching rhetoric" found in the theories of I. A. Richards, Kenneth Burke, and a "general semanticist approach" (120). Thus, it is clear that Fogarty, while not directly disparaging the stylistic elements of current-traditional rhetoric, implicitly suggested their inferiority to the "new or improved" theories of teaching rhetoric that he explored in *Roots for a New Rhetoric.*

In 1978, Young, building on Fogarty's work, labeled the current-traditional rhetoric a "paradigm" and suggested that "one important characteristic of current-traditional rhetoric is the exclusion of invention as a subdiscipline of the art" (32). In the same article, Young linked style with what he considered pejorative aspects of traditional rhetoric, such as grammar, correctness, and many of the same features described by Fogarty. In 1987, after the end of what is now considered composition's process period, Berlin continued this trajectory in *Rhetoric and Reality,* where he asserted that current-traditional rhetoric, which, he said, had appeared in response to the scientific curriculum at American universities, "makes the patterns of arrangement and superficial correctness the main ends of writing instruction." This emphasis, according to Berlin, conveyed the idea that invention "need not be taught since the business of the writer is to record careful observations or the reports of fellow observers" (9). Under Berlin's scenario, then, style became part of a mere "transcription process" in which the role of the writing instructor was regarded as "providing instruction in arrangement and style—arrangement so that the order of experience is correctly recorded, and style so that clarity is achieved and class affiliation established" (27). By suggesting that current-traditional rhetoric rendered invention unnecessary, and style elevated, Berlin not only advanced the invention agenda, but also renewed a long-time charge of style's elitist heritage, further undermining the status of an already maligned current-traditional paradigm.

Despite what seemed to be a gradual tendency to situate invention hierarchically over style, however, I suggest that style studies actually flourished during the process era, when many scholars linked the two canons in mutually productive ways. For example, in 1970, the NCTE Committee on the Nature of Rhetorical Invention stated, "One feature of [rhetorical invention] is that it *views 'style' as itself inventive*" (108; emphasis added). In an encyclopedic entry surveying the process era, Linda Vavra pointed out that "during the product/process paradigm shift of the 1970s and 1980s, stylistics flourished in composition's two arenas: reading/interpreting texts . . . and generating texts" (1998, 315). Depending on a person's philosophy of style, John Gage wrote in 1980, style can either be viewed as separate from invention "or it is one of the aspects of invention" (618). In his *Contemporary Rhetoric,* Ross Winterowd also suggested a unity of style and invention when he stated, "If one views theories of form and theories of style merely as sets of topics—which in most instances they are—then the whole process of composition is unified under the auspices of invention" (1975, 48). In their influential process-era text *Rhetoric: Discovery and Change,* famous for its invention heuristic, Young, Becker, and Pike (1970) highlighted the invention/style connection, which Young and Becker had explained in an earlier article: "In a complete theory, then, a particular style is a characteristic series of choices throughout the entire process of writing, including both discovery (invention) and linguistic selection and grouping (arrangement)" (Young and Becker 1967, 107). In all of these accounts, the authors viewed style and invention as connected in dynamic ways—not as part of the current-traditional rhetoric with which style has often been negatively associated.

While it is true historically that style and invention have always been separate canons of rhetoric, the tendency to characterize them as diametrically opposed, with few points of overlap, is a relatively recent phenomenon. According to Aristotle, as individual canons of rhetoric, invention and style have always been distinct at least in one respect: invention is considered the discovery of *ideas,* whereas style involves the discovery and use of *language* in certain contexts. Although invention can be generative, it is restricted to the formation of ideas, not language. Style, on the other hand, can be used both to discover and generate ideas through the improvisation of written language. Thus, the attempt to dichotomize style and invention reflects an incomplete characterization of the canons. Despite the dichotomization of the canons of style and invention by Fogarty, Berlin, and others, some scholars, both classical and modern, have attempted to find intersections among them (see, for example, Hawhee 2002). The idea that an "inventional style" exists, then, suggests the unique ability of style to facilitate the invention of ideas through writing. I assert that this productive idea of style, despite the revisionist tendency to characterize style as reductive, was dominant during the process era and must be reemphasized in any attempt to recuperate the study of style in composition today.

Part of the division between style and invention, both during and after the process era, is a long-standing theoretical split between content (that which is invented) and form (style and arrangement) that raises broader issues about the relationship between philosophy and rhetoric (Crowley 1990) and thought and language (Vygotsky 1997). The debate centers on whether style can be separated from meaning, a question which, if answered affirmatively, echoes what Lev Vygotsky calls a "metaphysical *disjunction* and *segregation*" of thought and language (Vygotsky 1997, 2). Adopting this "dualistic" view of a form-content split, often called the theory of "ornate form" (Milic 1965, 67), composition scholar Richard Ohmann argued that the very idea of style implies that the words written on a page can be different, or differently arranged, without a *necessary* corresponding difference in substance. According to Ohmann, the idea that by changing even one word, a writer changes, in turn, the entire meaning of a sentence "leads to the altogether counterintuitive conclusion that there can be no such thing as style" (1967, 141). In contrast to this dualistic view, the organic theory argues that form is *not* separable from content and that "a difference in style is always a difference in meaning" (Beardsley 1967, 199). The organic view supports the premise that language and thought necessarily coexist. According to this view, as Vygotsky states, there is an "*identification,* or *fusion,* of thought and speech" (1997, 2), which implies that content and form cannot be separated in achieving meaning.

While scholars like Ohmann and Richard Lanham have argued in favor of a view of style as "ornate form," it is clear that this dualistic theory has retained some of the negative connotations it acquired historically when sixteenth-century logician Peter Ramus attempted to confine rhetoric as a whole to the canons of style and delivery and associated invention with philosophy (see Ong 1974). Although no one has traced the overall impact of this schism on the composition field, it seems clear today that a view of style (or form) as separate from meaning (or content) has contributed to the association of the canon with a current-traditional paradigm which, according to Berlin and Inkster, views reality as fixed, knowable, and rational (Berlin and Inkster 1980, 4)—and unconcerned with invention or the production of new knowledge. The organic view of style, on the other hand, is seen as supporting Berlin's claim that language itself "embodies and generates knowledge" (Berlin 1987, 167), a central tenet of his social-epistemic rhetoric. This theoretical debate remains important today because it continues to influence what I suggest has become a fundamentally reductive view of style in composition and rhetoric and accounts in part for the neglect of attention to the study of style in the field.

While the form-content issue resurfaces regularly, as it did in a Stanley Fish op-ed column in the *New York Times* (see

Chap. 5), it was process-era composition scholars, aware of the apparent impasse the competing theories of style had produced, who proposed various compromises as a way to address the question. Milic, for example, suggested a practical solution based on the idea that "writing is a continuum leading from thought to expression" in which thought or content is "strongest at the origin," becomes "eventually coextensive" with form, and then gradually diminishes in importance as it approaches expression (where, ostensibly, form is more important). Milic felt that this continuum offered a way to keep form and content together, "yet separate for the process of analysis" (1975, 282). Virginia Tufte, in articulating a view of "grammar as style," argued that the feature of syntax, the predominant basis of her book, differs from diction in that changes in the former, in contrast to latter, "alter meaning, *if at all*, much less obviously" (1971, 6; emphasis added). Winterowd, recognizing the importance of the "manner/matter controversy" to composition pedagogy, suggested that two sentences with different forms "can both be taken as the same kind of speech act" and, therefore, as a matter of common sense, "two different sentences can share the same meaning" (1975, 271). Today, various language theories have shown that many factors beyond language itself contribute to meaning, and as such the form-content dichotomy does not hold the significance it once did. Nonetheless, the history—and persistence—of the debate clearly continue to influence recent discussions about the role of style in composition theory and pedagogy, as recurrent debates about the role of form, especially grammar, in composition demonstrate (see Chap. 5).

STYLE AS INNOVATION IN COMPOSITION'S PROCESS ERA

In establishing style as an innovative resource during the process era, it is important to note that several language theories and influences converged at the time to give rise to the hope of producing syntactic maturity among writers. It is clear, for instance, that Noam Chomsky's transformational linguistics

(Chomsky 1957; 1965) had an enormous influence. In fact, Frank O'Hare wrote that "Chomsky revolutionized grammatical theory" (O'Hare 1973, 5) and, indeed, transformational grammar was part of a general language-oriented milieu that influenced the development of such stylistic practices as generative rhetoric (Christensen 1963), sentence combining (O'Hare 1973; Mellon 1969, 1979; Bateman and Zidonis 1964), tagmemic rhetoric (Young *et al.* 1970), and a redeployment of classical rhetoric (Corbett 1971, 1989a, 1989b; Lanham 1974, 1976; Berthoff 1982), including the use of stylistic imitation. The work of these scholars helps refute the characterization of style as coming necessarily at the end of the composing process—generally as part of revision (Blakesley 1995, 193)—and invention coming earlier in that process. A revaluation of style in terms of its productive and inventive purposes earlier in the writing process can help re-establish the canon's rightful place in the recent history of composition studies. In this revaluation, a reanimation of style practices would have at least two purposes. First, it would offer composition scholars, teachers, and students access to and facility with a rich array of language resources that would allow them to gain expressive ability, eloquence, clarity, precision, and other valued "writerly" qualities. Secondly, a recuperation and reconsideration of style studies could aid writers with the invention of ideas.

The retrospective tendency to assume that style was unconnected to process or to emerging language theories seems to be widespread in the field today. Although there has been an attempt recently to account for the demise of the study of style around the mid-1980s (see, for example, Connors 2000), Joseph Williams and Rosemary Hake (1987) observed that style had come to be perceived as based on linguistic theories that relied, often exclusively, on the text, and made the sentence the highest hierarchical structure in a language system that includes a host of other relationships. These non-linguistic relationships were not only social and cultural, but also included units of discourse larger than the sentence (Roen 1996, 193). These factors, syntactic or otherwise, may explain in part the absence of any discussion of style in important works that look retrospectively at the process movement. One example of this type of work is the 1994 edited collection *Taking Stock: The Writing Process in the '90s*, an account of process that looks at expressivism but does not include any substantive mention of style. Several *Taking Stock* contributors, in fact, suggest that one of the most prominent features of the process era was its retrospective link to expressivist rhetoric. According to volume editor Lad Tobin, "Where the social constructivists and cultural critics come together with the traditionalists is in their criticism of expressivism and personal writing, and so that is where the critique of the writing process movement has been strongest" (6).

Yet, in his concern over the way expressivism has been constructed during the process movement, Tobin (1994) does not make reference to a theory of style that relates directly to expressivist notions. Labeled "individualist or psychological monism" by Louis Milic (1965), the theory is best summed up by the French aphorism, "Style is the man." The theory holds that a writer's style is the true expression of his or her personality and, therefore, no two writers can write the same way, rendering imitation impossible (Milic 1975, 222). That theory has been the most prevalent view of style throughout history. Yet, *Taking Stock*'s failure to acknowledge the influence of stylistic theories like psychological monism on the expressivist elements of process seems to disregard an opportunity to understand how the process movement constructed expressivist rhetoric and style in similarly reductive ways. For example, in the volume, Susan Wall (1994) writes that despite the continuing popularity of expressivist practices originating in process pedagogy, those practices are rejected today by compositionists with social views of language. Arguably, this retrojection occurs in much the same way that the process movement rejected current-traditional rhetoric and, at the same time, adopted some of the very practices of that rhetoric while giving them different names. Wall says:

> While the expressivist terms and practices of much process pedagogy have remained popular among many progressive elementary and secondary teachers—indeed, have been reinforced by later developments such as the whole language movement—a number of social-epistemic scholars have established their rhetorical ascendancy in college-level composition by rejecting the expressivism associated with the process movement (*just as the process movement established its claims by appealing to teachers to reject "current-traditionalism" in the name of a "new paradigm"*). (252; emphasis added)

Like Wall's association of an "expressivist menace" (Zebroski 1999, 99) with process and process with a new paradigm, I argue that the same phenomenon occurred with style and current-traditional rhetoric. In line with her argument, then, retrospective critiques conflate the notion of process with expressivism and of style with current-traditionalism and product, in both cases linking the terms with negative and reductive views of language. Tobin suggests that even though the link between personal writing and process is neither necessary nor accurate, the two are often "linked in practice and perception" (6). Similarly, a closer examination suggests that Tobin and his contributors, including such composition scholars as Ken Macrorie, Peter Elbow, James Moffett, James Britton, and Donald Murray, seem to consider certain aspects of style a part of product. Evidence of this phenomenon can be found when Tobin first defines process as "an *emphasis* on the process, student choice and voice, revision, self-expression," and then, in contrast, goes on to define what process ostensibly is working against: "a critique (or even outright rejection) of traditional, product-driven, rules-based, correctness-obsessed writing instruction" (5). While Tobin does not mention the word "style" explicitly in this context, he places stylistic "prose models" on a list that also includes "grammar lessons" and "lectures on usage" in his narrative of "life before the writing process movement" (2–4).

While the association of style with words like "product," "traditional," "rules," and "correctness" (see Crowley 1989) leads to its close affiliation with "grammar" and renders it retrospectively counter to the aims of the process movement, what Phelps calls the generally more "progressive" aspects of writing have not escaped reductive views, either (Phelps 1999, 42). As a matter of fact, both ends of the dichotomy—process and product, invention and style—have been viewed unevenly by the field. Crowley (1990) demonstrates this point in *The Methodical Memory: Invention in Current-Traditional Rhetoric,* where she suggests that rhetorical invention "goes in and out of fashion because it is intimately tied to current developments in ethics, politics, and the epistemology of whatever culture it serves" (1). Clearly, this tendency is, in part, what prompted the recent resurrection of invention in volumes such as Janet Atwill and Janice Lauer's *Perspectives on Rhetorical Invention* (2002) and Anis Bawarshi's *Genre and the Invention of the Writer* (2003), both of which tie invention to current cultural developments in significant ways. It suggests the way in which invention has, as Crowley suggests, resurfaced because of cultural concerns about writing.

Despite her argument that invention has been devalued at various times in history, however, Crowley makes a hierarchical distinction that seems to place invention over style. After suggesting that in "modern rhetoric, attention to invention has been overshadowed by interest in arrangement and style" (Crowley 1990, 1), she makes the Ramistic move of separating style from invention. Under this scenario, Crowley perpetuates a division whose roots stem from the sixteenth-century logician Peter Ramus's separation of invention and arrangement (which he categorizes as logic) from style and delivery (which he includes under the province of rhetoric; see Chap. 2). For her part, Crowley suggests that invention alone is important culturally, while style (along with arrangement) becomes the reductive equivalent of what she calls "linguistic techniques":

> To teach writing as though the composing process begins with arrangement or style, then, assumes that speakers and writers can

> deploy discourse in a cultural and ethical vacuum. . . . Composition becomes the manipulation of words for its own sake. (Crowley 1990, 168)

It is evident that, at least in this context, Crowley views style as a mere surface feature or ornament of current-traditional rhetoric, not connected to the epistemic realm in which she situates invention. In using this construction, Crowley fails to attribute to style a richer view as knowledge-making and connected to invention, philosophy, culture, and rhetoric.

STYLE IN THE PRODUCTION OF LANGUAGE

In contrast to constructions of style as merely "surface" or "ornamental" features, I contend that during style's renaissance in the 1960s and for parts of the next two decades, composition scholars saw the possibility of using stylistic techniques to increase a writer's repertoire of language resources and, ultimately, to improve writing abilities. In particular, Chomsky's transformational grammar was seen as offering a possible means, through the study of syntax, of fostering what he called the "creative aspect" of language, or "the ability of speakers to produce and understand sentences they have never encountered before" (Riley and Parker 1998, 222). This applied to student writing in terms of arguing that syntax is a great source of both variety and deviation in written English. In line with Chomsky's work, then, one of the predominant syntactic methods of the process period was sentence combining, a technique whose goal is to improve syntactic maturity. As Connors suggests in "The Erasure of the Sentence" (2000), two other important techniques included generative rhetoric and imitation.

Beyond Connors, whose sentence rhetorics address just part of the stylistic work during that period, other experiments with rhetorical aspects of style are examined, such as Young, Becker, and Pike's tagmemic rhetoric; Corbett's amplification and Lanham's classical tropes and figures; and Christensen's generative rhetoric. The contrast in these practices is important in that the language-based approaches correspond with improving the fluent command of varied stylistic resources, especially syntactic ones; the others, in contrast, are connected with the rhetorical *use* of these resources. In both instances, the dynamic theories and practices are a vital part of the process period and suggest a use that has often been overlooked in accounts of the Golden Age. It is significant that the tendency has been to write many of these practices out of the history of the period.

TAGMEMIC STYLE

Perhaps no one else during the 1970s articulated the importance of an inventive style more clearly than the trio of Young, Becker, and Pike. In "Toward a Modern Theory of Rhetoric: A Tagmemic Contribution," Young and Becker (1967), relying in part on Pike's development of tagmemics as a field of linguistics, argued that style should be looked at as more than merely a deviation from the norm and should include not only the prewriting process, but all other aspects of the writing process as well: "In a complete theory, then, a particular style is a characteristic series of choices throughout the *entire process of writing, including both discovery (invention)* and *linguistic selection and grouping (arrangement)*" (Young and Becker 1967, 107; emphasis added). Berlin stated in his book *Rhetoric and Reality* that for Young and Becker "form and content are one." Perhaps more important, Berlin recognized that Young and Becker saw arrangement and style as intricately related to invention: "In their view," Berlin stated, "discussions of arrangement and style are finally discussions of invention" (1987, 171). Young and Becker developed this theory of an "inventional style" in an overall concept that they called "the universe of discourse":

> A writer's style, we believe, is the characteristic route he takes through all the choices presented in both the writing and prewriting stages. It is the manifestation of his conception of the topic modified by his audience, situation, and intention—what we might call his "universe of discourse." (Young and Becker 1967, 140)

Clearly, then, Young and Becker did not see style as something "added on" at the end of the writing process or as separate from content. For them, it was an integral part of every facet of rhetoric and central to any successful writing activity; stated differently, it was a quintessential part of the process movement.

While Young, Becker, and Pike (1970) are often cited for the notion of "tagmemic invention"—which relies on a theory of particle, wave, and field—at the center of their text, *Rhetoric: Discovery and Change*, their broad conception of style, which they defined as a "way of behaving," is not as well known. A key aspect of their redefinition of style was their emphasis on its epistemological implications: the fact that it helps form the content of any product at each stage of the writing *process*:

> When people think of a writer's style, they usually think of the distinctive features of his prose—a distinctive lexicon and syntax and, less often, a distinctive subject matter. That is, style is conventionally defined in terms of characteristics of the finished work. While granting that this concept of style is at times useful, we want to offer an alternative that emphasizes instead what one does as he is writing. We propose to view style as a particular way of behaving. Our focus, then, is on characteristics of the process of writing rather than on characteristics of the product. (359)

Although not going against traditional conceptions of style, Young, Becker, and Pike nevertheless proposed a new view of the writer as a "creator" who "must see the art of rhetoric in dynamic terms, as search and choice, as a way of behaving." Already allying themselves in 1970 with more social views of writing, the authors saw the writer as one "concerned with formulating elements of experience and ordering them in coherent and meaningful systems, with formulating his relationship with his readers, and with shaping the notions welling up in his mind into a verbal object" (360). Their view of style as social, rhetorical, and inventional suggested its close affiliation with today's popular conceptions of the process of writing.

In what can only be seen as an anticipation of Carolyn Miller's characterization of genre theory (Miller 1984), Young, Becker, and Pike also described the development of what they called an "intelligent style," or "an ability to isolate and identify the problems inherent in the activity of writing and to move toward workable solutions deliberately" (Young *et al.* 1970, 360). They suggested that writers must have a concept of writing problems that they view both generically and specifically and then adopt heuristic procedures that allow the intelligent stylist to "behave in new situations as if he has been there before." The problem-based approach made style much more than a static element of the writing process. As Young, Becker, and Pike. described it, "By conceiving of the process of writing as a search for solutions to an interrelated sequence of problems and by providing heuristic procedures as guides in this search, we have sought to provide the tools necessary to form an intelligent style or reform an unintelligent one" (360–61). Clearly, they viewed style and invention as part of a dynamic process of writing in which the two canons, both parts of an "interrelated sequence of problems," are inseparable. Furthermore, the authors connected style and inventional problem solving in a way that anticipated the cognitive-based rhetoric of Linda Flower and John Hayes (1981), which evolved at a slightly later point of the process era.

In their view of style as part of an overall rhetoric that includes invention and arrangement, Young and Becker (1967) challenged some of the countervailing characterizations of style as the defining feature of current-traditional rhetoric and a product-based paradigm. Rather, in their view, style was one important element of their overall rhetorical theory of "tagmemics." Traditionally, they explain, style, while borrowing from a foundation of grammar, went beyond that foundation to explore how language could be used in various rhetorical situations:

> Style, the third of the rhetorical arts in classical rhetoric, was largely the technique of framing effective sentences. Its function was to give clarity, force, and beauty to ideas. Although grammar was its

> foundation, style was clearly a separate art, concerned with the effective use of language rather than simply with the correct use. (83)

Young and Becker went on to explain that style could become an end in itself, "at times preempting the entire field of rhetoric" (84), partly because of the theoretical division of form from content. Addressing what Milic refers to as the dualistic view of language, the authors considered the separation of form from content in both arrangement and style a serious deficiency. They observed, "Both the art of arrangement and the art of style divorce form from content, *failing to consider the importance of the act of discovery in the shaping of form*" (85; emphasis added). Thus, they were especially concerned that seeing style as merely a deviation from the norm has the effect of treating conventional language as "styleless language": mere embellishment with no connection to invention (106). They indicated the importance of style's inventive qualities in the discovery of language, a vital role that few others acknowledged explicitly, either during the process era or later in the retrospective accounts of that period.

CLASSICAL RHETORIC

Despite Corbett's general recognition for his innovative work in recuperating the study of style during the 1970s and 1980s, his work in classical rhetoric is not often associated specifically with composition's process era. In many respects, his theories of style constituted a very real part of style's Golden Age, yet he never made the explicit connection between style and invention that seems to exist, at least implicitly, in many aspects of his work. For example, Corbett made no more than a reference to the importance of an inventional style when he retraced the "threefold implication" of *lexis*, the Greek word for style, in which "we take the *thoughts* collected by invention and put them into *words* for the *speaking out* in delivery" (Corbett 1971, 414). I contend that Corbett's failure to make the explicit connection between style and invention has resulted in his work on style sometimes being overlooked as an integral part of the process era in which it is clearly situated.

One specific area where Corbett alluded to the reciprocal effect that invention and style had on each other was in his brief discussion of classical amplification, or extenuation, which he defined as the process of highlighting, or making "as big as possible," the points made in speech or writing (Corbett 1971, 334). Corbett wrote that "the invention of matter . . . eventually had its effect on style when there developed a great interest in amplification" (1989a, 144). Classical scholar Douglas Kelly has suggested that amplification "provides the author with modal or formal techniques by which to achieve topical invention" (Kelly 1978, 245). Indeed, the idea that amplification invents a liminal space that exists between "figures of speech" and "figures of thought" places it at the very intersection between style and invention during the "new classicism" of the process era. As rhetorical scholar Don Paul Abbott (2001) explains, in classical rhetoric, amplification was an important part of copiousness or "copie," whose various meanings include variation, abundance or richness, eloquence, and the ability to vary language and thought. According to Abbott, "amplification was, in effect, the active implementation of imitation. As such, the process combined the classical divisions of invention, style, and arrangement" (162). It is clear that Corbett saw amplification as a means of producing *copia* because of the variety of expression it produces. Even though he never used the idea explicitly to connect style and invention, however, he did acknowledge that "*copia* was partly a matter of fertile invention and partly a matter of stylistic resourcefulness" (Corbett 1989a, 131). In certain indirect ways, then, one can infer that Corbett regarded the intersection of invention and style as the fertile ground of language resources.

While Corbett saw invention and style as separate, but equally important, canons of rhetoric, Lanham attributed to style an importance that few others do, stating that composition's "natural subject is style" (1974, 14). In *Style: An Anti-Textbook*, Lanham (1974) observed, "Writing courses usually stress, not style, but rhetoric's other two traditional parts, finding arguments and arranging them" (131). Lanham added, however, "*Yet both, implicit in a study of style, emerge naturally only from a concentration on it*" (13–14; emphasis added). In placing style ahead of invention and arrangement in his version of the rhetorical hierarchy, Lanham suggested that "style itself must be the object of contemplation" (14). Like Corbett, Lanham also turned to classical rhetoric as the source of his recuperative effort, where he drew upon rhetorical tropes and figures. Lanham's placement of style first in the canonical hierarchy began a theme of reversal that runs throughout his work and continues into his most recent book (Lanham 2006).

In his focus on style, rather than on invention, as the primary rhetorical canon, Lanham adopted the view that "rhetorical man is trained not to discover reality but to manipulate it" (1976, 4). He contrasted this rhetorical view with the "serious" view of a transparent style whose objective is the efficient communication of "facts, concepts, or imitations of reality" (1). According to Lanham, it is important to look self-consciously *at* the stylistic surface—what he called the opaque style—rather than *through* style to an underlying reality where a transparent content is normally thought to exist. He stated that he discovered this idea while studying the rhetorical language in Sir Philip Sidney's *Old Arcadia*:

> He was trying to glimpse a world where verbal ornament is as essential as essence, as serious as serious purpose, and as needful for man, and where ornament and essence, like systole and diastole, like breathing out and breathing in, constitute the life-giving oscillation of human life. (Lanham 1983b, 58)

Borrowing from one of Burke's ideas in *Counter-Statement* (1968), Lanham argued that style reverses our normal way of thinking about what constitutes reality. "Style," he wrote, "instead of creating the decorative surface of reality, may be reality's major constituent element" (Lanham 1983b, 77). Lanham elaborated on this idea in his discussion of the virtues of the opaque style:

> The opaque styles, then, imply a reality, a self, a pattern of attention, and a range of motive different from those usually called "serious" but equally necessary to our own full reality. When put in a behavioral context they reverse the whole direction of thinking about style. The tail seems to have been wagging the dog all along. (1983b, 76)

For Lanham, in "a world where words determine thoughts" (140), style is an essential part of "man as fundamentally a role player" who is motivated to play not only for advantage but also for pleasure (1976, 4–5). Style, then, becomes an important element of "play" and "game" through language, and it is through verbal play, said Lanham, that style should be studied and taught. Lanham's idea of style-as-play placed his aesthetic approach to language in line with several theories of the period, including deconstruction. His view of style as more than a transparent medium countered a tradition of plain style, clarity, and the conception of style as inseparable from content. Lanham argued convincingly that focusing on the stylistic surface and the play of language as ornament can, in itself, give students important language resources. He suggested that people should experiment with "hypotaxis" and "parataxis," with "periodic" and "running" style, and with the iconography of style (an apparent precursor to today's visual rhetoric as well as Lanham's interest in hypertext as reflected in his book *The Electronic Word* 1993). In all pertinent ways, he suggested, style can help generate ideas, confirming his notion that style can, through the use of language, be inventive. Lanham is perhaps one of the only recent scholars to assume that style is *the* indispensable rhetorical canon that cannot be ignored, a position that has never been considered seriously by the field.

GENERATIVE RHETORIC

In "A Generative Rhetoric of the Sentence," the main articulation of his views on the subject, Christensen (1963) set forth his ideas for how to help students develop a mature style. In part, Christensen was attempting to address his belief that "in composition courses, we do not really teach our captive charges to write better—we merely *expect* them to" (F. Christensen and B. Christensen 1978, 25). Christensen's central premise of sentence maturity can be summed up in writer John Erksine's statement: "You make a point, not by subtracting as though you sharpened a pencil, but by adding" (26). Thus, in order to help writers develop a mature style, Christensen began with the principle of "addition," by which he meant adding sentence modifiers of different lengths—which he called "free modifiers"—to base clauses that are often short. Sentences composed of base clauses and free modifiers are called "cumulative sentences," which he said function according to four principles: addition, the direction of modification, levels of generality, and texture. Christensen explained the process further:

> The main clause, which may or may not have a sentence modifier before it, advances the discussion; but the additions placed after it move backward, as in this clause, to modify the statement of the main clause or more often to explicate it or exemplify it, so that the sentence has a flowing and ebbing movement, advancing to a new position and then pausing to consolidate it, leaping and lingering as the popular ballad does. (F. Christensen and B. Christensen 1978, 27–28)

As Richard Coe indicates, Christensen's use of free modifiers has a particular function in generating a recursive language process:

> The most "natural" place to add a "loose" or free modifier . . . is in the postmodifier slot, located after the noun or verb it modifies. Physically, the sentence keeps moving across the page, but cognitively/rhetorically, the sentence pauses. As the modifier attaches to a preceding base, the "movement" or "direction of modification" is back toward that noun or verb "head." (Coe 1998, 133)

While the intended outcomes of Christensen's syntactic emphasis have been explored, few scholars have noted another important feature of these structures: the cognitive importance of being able to articulate relationships among concepts and phenomena. Thus, for Christensen, the use of generative rhetoric to develop maturity in writing worked in the sense that syntax forms a number of varying relationships—those between agent, action, and object of the action; logical, spatial, chronological, and hierarchical relationships; and "given" and "new" elements of a sentence, to name a few. The idea in generative rhetoric is that these various aspects of syntax reflect and, in turn, may catalyze cognitive maturation toward more complex thought. In other words, the use of syntax in the form of cumulative sentences presumably allows the writer to express more complex ideas and relationships, which is what makes writing "better" or more mature.

For Christensen, the word "generative" was important in suggesting that form can be used in the invention and production of language. "We need a rhetoric of the sentence," he observed, "that will do more than combine the ideas of primer sentences. We need one that will *generate* ideas" (F. Christensen and B. Christensen 1978, 26). Coe (1998) indicated that the idea of generating content includes invention: "The crux of Christensen's generative rhetoric is the use of form—especially syntax—to generate content (i.e., not just as *dispositio*, but also as a technique for *inventio*)" (131). He further explained the idea of the generative nature of form in his influential *College English* article, "An Apology for Form; Or, Who Took the Form out of the Process": "Form, in its emptiness, is heuristic, for it guides a structured search. Faced with the emptiness of a form, a human being seeks matter to fill it. Form becomes, therefore, a motive for generating information" (Coe 1987, 18). Indeed, as Coe suggested, Christensen's own language indicated that he intended a connection between style and invention. In "The Generative Rhetoric of the Sentence," originally published in 1963, Christensen wrote, "The idea of levels of structure urge[s] the student to add further levels to what he has already produced, so that *the structure itself becomes an aid to discovery*" (1978, 24; emphasis added).

Christensen's rhetoric becomes inventive in the sense that writers can build upon the base clause in a way that allows them to generate further ideas. In "A Generative Rhetoric of the Sentence," Christensen (1978) explained this inventional process:

> The main clause . . . exhausts the mere fact of the idea: logically there is nothing more to say. The additions stay with the same idea, probing its bearings and implications, exemplifying it or seeking an analogy or metaphor for it, or reducing it to details. Thus the mere form of the sentence generates ideas. It serves the needs of both the writer and the reader, the writer by compelling him to examine his thought, the reader by letting him into the writer's thought. (6)

For Christensen, the cumulative sentence, with its principle of addition that involves right-branching and left-branching sentences, was a key part of writing dynamic sentences "representing the mind thinking" and forcing the writer to explore the implications of an idea—that is, to "amplify" that idea. In this sense, the very form of the sentence, considered by Christensen to be an essential part of its style, is productive; as a heuristic, it becomes part of invention. Berlin (1987) acknowledged the importance of generative rhetoric during the process era when he wrote that Christensen "taught writing teachers something about the relation of form to meaning, especially the ways in which linguistic forms can themselves generate meaning" (136).

SENTENCE COMBINING

Even though Christensen (1978) eschewed any connection between generative rhetoric and sentence combining, there are, in fact, many points of intersection between the two practices. As William Stull (1985) has suggested, "Sentence combining and generative rhetoric work towards the same ends: syntactic maturity as evidenced by good original writing" (84). Stull adds that he sees the possibility that a synthesis of the two would prove synergistic:

> Each method may well enhance the other. To sentence-combining practice, the generative rhetoric adds a conceptual framework. To Christensen's four principles of style, sentence combining gives specific application. Where sentence combining enhances students' written fluency, generative rhetoric enhances their sense of style. (85)

Despite Stull's claim that there are a number of points of intersection between the two practices, there are also differences. Whereas generative rhetoric is based on structural grammar, sentence combining originates in Chomsky's transformational-generative grammar. While generative rhetoric is based on Christensen's principles of addition, direction of modification, levels of generality, and texture, sentence combining uses techniques of embedding, deletion, subordination, and coordination. The practice of sentence combining benefited from several early studies. Probably, the most important was that of Kellogg Hunt, who discovered that a good indicator of maturity in writing was the length of clauses, "what I will describe as one main clause plus whatever subordinate clauses happen to be attached to or embedded within it" (Hunt 1965, 305). In assessing stylistic maturity, Hunt found that a reliable indicator was something he developed and called the "minimal terminable unit" or "T-unit." Each T-unit, he suggested, is "minimal in length, and each could be terminated grammatically between a capital and a period" (306). In other words, T-units are units of syntax that can be punctuated as complete sentences, and Hunt's idea is that students should be able to write longer T-units at the end of the semester than at the beginning (see Halloran and Whitburn 1982, 59–60).

On the basis of Chomskyan theory, sentence combining drew on differences between deep and surface structures in language that have been useful in stylistic analysis. Both the deep and surface structures of a sentence have proven significant. If it is true, as Chomsky argued, that the deep structures (relational patterns) of a language can generate an indefinite number of understandable statements (surface structures), then the very act of choosing among—or generating choice among—numerous possibilities itself involves an inventive process, that is, a process of choice and creation. This is an extremely generative aspect of sentence combining that many sentence-combining adherents did not articulate as forcefully as Christensen did, but that exists nonetheless.

At the same time, however, it is clear that scholars have established a connection between the principles of Chomsky's generative-transformational grammar and the improvement in student writing. In particular, as O'Hare stated, the Bateman and Zidonis study in the 1970s established the authors' claim that "a knowledge of generative grammar enabled students to increase significantly the proportion of well-formed sentences they wrote and to increase the complexity without sacrificing the grammaticality of their sentences" (O'Hare 1973, 6). O'Hare pointed out that John Mellon's study, reported in *Transformational Sentence-Combining*, essentially reached the same conclusion. In both instances, O'Hare stated, the evidence was compelling, but ultimately inconclusive: "Although it is at least questionable whether it was a knowledge of generative grammar that led Bateman and Zidonis's students to write more mature sentences, it is not unreasonable to assume that something in their experimental treatment must have caused those students to write more maturely" (18). The final report of the project in 1970 described more fully the circumstances in which students studied and transformed their style and also made several prescient recommendations regarding the study of style in composition.

When Mellon argued in "Issues in the Theory and Practice of Sentence-Combining: A Twenty-Year Perspective" that "sentence-combining covers arrangement and style but not invention," he adhered to the classical separation of each of the canons. Yet, in stating that a writing class structured around sentence combining "could be better still were the sentence-combining lessons paired with lessons on invention and the structure of argument" (Mellon 1979, 29), Mellon did not acknowledge the generative, and potentially inventional, aspects of sentence combining itself. This is not to say, of course, that Mellon did not recognize that invention and style are related to each other. I argue, however, that he has not given full credit to the practice that he had such an integral role in designing. Furthermore, his position confirms the tendency, as Winterowd argued, to see sentence combining as simply a series of exercises, divorced from a true rhetorical context. This is the precise critique made by Elbow (1985), who argued that the concentration on syntax in sentence combining is ultimately harmful as a generative tool:

> I think sentence-combining is vulnerable to attack for being so a-rhetorical—so distant from the essential process of writing. In sentence-combining the student is not engaged in figuring out what she wants to say or saying what is on her mind. And because it provides prepackaged words and ready-made thoughts, sentence-combining reinforces the push-button, fast food expectations in our culture. (233)

In contrast to Elbow's claim, I argue that sentence combining has essentially been unfairly misunderstood, even by some of its practitioners. Mellon did not link sentence combining with invention in his 1979 article, which many saw as the final word on sentence combining. However, sentence-combining articles and research continued until the mid-1980s, and as the seven new editions of *The Writer's Options* demonstrated, scholars attempted to place sentence combining within a rhetorical context. When Shirley K. Rose (1983) suggested, however, that sentence combining was not a new practice but was part of a number of similar practices that had originated in the eighteenth and nineteenth centuries, her historical survey did not include anything about the inventive, generative, or rhetorical aspects of that practice. It seems clear that those who took up Chomsky's generative-transformational grammar as the foundation for sentence combining did not give full credit to his theories as the basis of inventive language processes. For that reason, I argue, sentence combining has been misinterpreted in the overall retrospective account of the process era and has not been given a fully comprehensive evaluation in its role as a feature of inventive, generative, and rhetorical language production.

SIGNIFICANCE FOR COMPOSITION STUDIES

It is important to observe how certain parts of composition history acquire intellectual pedigrees that can be difficult to change. One example of such a phenomenon is composition's process movement, retrospective accounts of which are beginning to be scrutinized as scholars question the way process is now described or defined. For example, Tobin and Newkirk (1994) express concerns with the retrojection of expressivism and, in *Taking Stock*, question the way this movement gets pejoratively labeled after the fact as the central aspect of the process era. Johnson (2003) has identified the same trend in his reexamination of a renegade rhetoric that he sees as misinterpreted in composition scholarship of the past few decades. Connors (2000) writes of a similar occurrence when he revalues sentence rhetorics in "The Erasure of the Sentence." Importantly, the process of retrojection has also figured prominently in the fate of stylistic study in rhetoric and composition. In fact, I argue that the retrospective affiliation of style with a much-maligned current-traditional rhetoric has ultimately resulted in the loss of a rich reservoir of resources which, as this chapter has shown, were deployed with great success during composition's process era. These stylistic resources are intimately connected with invention and suggest ways of generating language and ideas in productive ways. Indeed, the resources of style offer ways to revalue practices like amplification, generative rhetoric, sentence combining, and tagmemic rhetoric for writers. As Connors (2000) suggests in his analysis of sentence combining—one that applies to all the stylistic techniques I explore here—nothing has ever shown that these stylistic practices do not aid in developing language maturity or fluency. In other words, these techniques are effective in developing a writer's style.

In any revaluation of an inventional style that developed during the process era, however, an important question remains: What is at stake in reanimating the study of style as an important part of process? As a field, what do we gain by reclaiming stylistic practices from the process era even if they are inextricably linked to invention and other dynamic features of language use? First, in doing so, composition gives itself a reason for rehabilitating the study of style as a topic of serious scholarly inquiry. As it stands, the absence of style from retrospective accounts of the process period very likely reflects the desire to avoid any pejorative affiliation of the term "style" with current-traditional rhetoric and its connection to grammar and usage, the use of models or forms, and other practices that have acquired "baggage" in the field over time. Yet, even if this stylistic taboo is lifted, how is the recuperation of style as a vital part of process helpful today? One benefit, I argue, is in reestablishing a close nexus between style and invention, which is worthwhile as we look at the tools available for analyzing discourse. Because style has come to be thought of generally as a static canon that is deployed only at the *end* of the writing process, it has been difficult to imagine it as a vital way to generate language—as a resource for constructing language and discovering new ideas through writing. In reestablishing style's connection with invention, those concerns are now allayed, paving the way for a new inventional style as part of composition practice.

Another advantage may seem less obvious at first. The stylistic options mentioned in this chapter represent some of the process-era language practices in use during that time. While some may still be used in composition classrooms, I suggest that most are not, and certainly not to the same extent. Imagine the possibilities that exist in renewing these stylistic resources as seen through the lens of their inventive qualities. If these are reclaimed today with an eye toward their potential use in generating language and ideas through writing, a real renaissance of stylistic discovery could be in store for composition theory, practice, and pedagogy. This chapter has shown that style's exclusion from the field results, at heart, from an accidental affiliation with current-traditional rhetoric that denies the inventional aspects of stylistic techniques. Given the field's turn toward social and public forms of writing, the advantages of an inventional style are clear. It seems that the time is ripe to bring the study of style, out of style for so long, back into the reservoir of language resources that process-era scholars recognized as crucial to the language theories and innovations of the time.

4

STYLE IN THE DIASPORA OF COMPOSITION STUDIES

Around 1985, after two decades of innovative activity, the study of style became largely invisible in the hegemonic research scholarship in composition and rhetoric and has remained so ever since. Just as the study of style is largely invisible in the field today, however, it is, paradoxically, ubiquitous, and evidence of its continued presence can be found in many diverse places in the discipline. In *The New St. Martin's Guide to Teaching Writing*, Robert Connors and Cheryl Glenn (1999) contend that "style has diffused today into one of the most important canons of rhetoric" (232) and go on to list a few places where it can be found: in personal and business writing; "lurking" behind areas of critical theory like deconstruction, which shares with style the search and play of tropes, and reader-response literary criticism, including Stanley Fish's (1980) "affective stylistics"; and in "socioeconomic ramifications of style," such as cultural critic Kenneth Cmiel's (1990) economic rationale for the development of the plain style. Importantly, however, style in its dispersed form is often not *called* style, but instead is named something else within the field. Janice Lauer (2002) suggests that this same phenomenon has occurred with rhetorical invention which, she says, exists today in a "diaspora" of composition studies, areas where that canon has "migrated, entered, settled, and shaped many other areas of theory and practice in rhetoric and composition." Like invention, I argue, work on style has also migrated to composition's so-called "diaspora," where it is "implicit, fragmented" and located in many areas of inquiry (2).[1]

In "Rhetorical Invention: The Diaspora," Lauer (2002) investigates what has happened to studies of rhetorical invention, a central part of what she calls "'past' composition studies" from the 1960s to the mid-1980s. During that period, which corresponds with composition's process movement and the Golden Age of style, a number of publications focused explicitly on invention theory and pedagogy. In light of the dearth of work that has appeared since that time, Lauer asks what has happened to studies of invention in the field. In response, she draws a parallel to the medieval period (from the fourth to the fourteenth centuries) and argues that like then "invention today can be found in a diaspora of composition areas rather than in discussions labeled 'invention'" (2). In addition to enumerating several scholarly emphases that have been marginalized since the mid-1980s—for example, the relationship between invention and the writing process—Lauer looks to a number of sites where she contends the diffusion of invention studies has occurred: writing in the disciplines and across the curriculum; public contexts and cultural studies; studies of gender, race, and cultural difference; theories of technology; studies of genre; and hermeneutics. From her survey of these areas, Lauer concludes that recent work on invention in the field is now "dispersed and localized, precluding any final characterization of a unified theory or common set of practices" (11).

In adopting the concept of the diaspora, Lauer borrows a term rich in history and significance. Although Lauer's use of the word denotes the more generic meaning of a flight (of a group) from a country or region—or a "dispersion"—the term *diaspora* initially referred specifically to the Jewish population around the Mediterranean that was forced to live outside of Palestine after the Babylonian invasion. Since then, the term has been used by the African-American community to refer to the "forced migration" of groups from Africa under threat (Himley 2003), and other groups have adopted the term as well, leading to the development of a separate area of scholarship known as Diasporic Studies. While Lauer does not complicate the notion of diaspora in this way, such a use is not inconsistent with her thinking about the fate of invention in composition. I propose that the idea of a "forced migration" applies not only to the canon of invention in the aftermath of the process era, but also—and even more urgently—to the study of style during that same period. Lauer sees the diapora as a "promising terrain" for future studies in composition, and this is no less the case if we view the dispersion of style as a forced exile from the discipline.

While Lauer's idea of the diaspora opens up many possibilities, it does not address potential explanations for this migration. In *The Ecology of Composition*, Margaret Syverson (1999) proposes one when she suggests that dynamic changes in writing theory exist as part of an "ecology" of composition studies. Syverson's theory is important in explaining the highly dynamic nature of style and the way in which its migration as a topic into other spaces of composition studies suggests a corresponding evolution in its use by scholars: "Emergent properties suggest that all of our classification systems are actually open-ended, explanatory theories rather than closed, deterministic containers" (11). Syverson proposes a way that we may want to view style as it has emerged in various sites of the diaspora. Part of the "ecology" is that "as new forms or agents emerge, others fall away, break up, dwindle down, rust, decay, or decompose into either chaotic or stable states from which new forms emerge" (11–12).

The implication of Syverson's theoretical approach is that the understanding of style in composition has not remained static in *a priori* locations but has developed dynamically as it encounters language and practices in other areas of the field (see Hopper 1998). Syverson's theory also helps explain that the view of style I am proposing is not that of language as a container to be filled; even during the heyday of stylistic studies during the modern Golden Age, composition scholars working in style studies rejected that approach, envisioning style instead as a dynamic canon of rhetoric (see, for example, Young *et al.* 1970; Corbett 1976; Lanham 1974, 1983a; Christensen 1963; Bateman and Zidonis 1970). One distinction that I make, however, is that the concept of an emerging style remains grounded in rhetoric. It is possible that various language resources may be deployed to generate the new forms Syverson mentions, but the basic tools of that undertaking remain rhetorical styles. Thus, for example, some of the "forms" or "agents" that may be seen as breaking up or decaying might include the use of a high or elegant style that was common in the time of Cicero or the use of periodic sentences. Yet, in the evolution of these rhetorical components, it is important that even those that are no longer regularly used remain a part of overall stylistic resources. Syverson seems to affirm this premise when she writes that "the concept of emergence is not in opposition to entropy; it includes it" (11).

GENRE THEORY

One reason for beginning with genre as a site of dispersion is that, like style, it is an area that has traditionally been ignored in first-year composition pedagogy, though it does appear in professional and technical communication. Amy Devitt (1997) alludes to a connection between style and genre when she writes, "If the metaphoric and literal connection of genre as language standard has illuminated the role of constraint/standardization and choice/variation, then perhaps it can illuminate the place of genre in the writing classroom" (54). Yet, she fails to make an explicit connection between genre and stylistic analysis. For example, while using the relationship of variation versus constraint, choice versus standards in order to redefine genres as dynamic and shifting, she does not point out that style itself functions as a dynamic set of relationships. Similarly, when Lauer describes the movement of invention into a "diaspora" of composition studies, she does not ask the critical question of what accounts for its diffusion into other areas of interest in the field. In the case of style, it seems crucial to account for its continuing neglect as a dynamic language theory. I propose that one reason for style's migration is that it has acquired a certain amount of cultural "baggage" that has resulted in compositionists' distancing themselves from the discourse of style.

In this instance, Lauer's concept of the diaspora seems more of a forced migration than an emergent property of language development.

An example of style's migration can be found in Anis Bawarshi's (2003) *Genre and the Invention of the Writer*, where the author identifies the composition syllabus as a "site of invention" in which genre is taking place in a dynamic way. In his book, Bawarshi examines the way in which genres constitute writers into subject formations and position the writer as someone who is "written" or produced by the genres he or she writes (11). In a chapter in which he looks at various classroom genres—the syllabus, the writing prompt, and the student essay—Bawarshi makes the argument that the first-year writing classroom "is a multilayered, multitextured site of social and material action and identity formation, a site that is reproduced as it is rhetorically enacted by its participants within the various classroom genres available to them" (14–15). In examining the syllabus as one genre that contributes to this multilayered site, Bawarshi suggests that the frequent dichotomy of "you" and "we" in the syllabi of composition instructors reflects "on the pronoun level a larger tension many teachers face . . . between establishing solidarity with students and demarcating lines of authority" (122).

Bawarshi's analysis of the way in which teachers use pronouns to position students as "passive recipients" and to effect a contractual obligation draws upon the work of Louis Althusser (1971) and the power dynamic of interpellation. Althusser suggests that ideology interpellates individuals as subjects in a way that appears to be consensual, so that individuals seem to choose a subject position that is actually imposed upon them. Bawarshi argues that the use of the pronouns "you" and "we" in the syllabus serves, in Althusserian fashion, to "hail" students as subjects:

> This "you," coupled with the occasional "we," the second most common pronoun, works as a hailing gesture, interpellating the

> individual who walks into the classroom as a student subject, one who then becomes part of the collective "we" that will operationalize this activity system we call the FYW course. (Bawarshi 2003, 123–24)

While Bawarshi is able to show convincingly that pronouns function in a power dynamic that results in an inherent hierarchy among instructors and students, I argue that by using direct tools of stylistic analysis, he would have had access to additional resources to understand the rhetorical and generic forces at work in syllabus construction.

For example, a fuller stylistic analysis would help to show how the social relationships implicit in the use of pronouns change the dynamics at work in the syllabus as a genre. While Bawarshi explains the pronoun tension within the ideological framework of interpellation, I argue that it is actually the same "tension" between exophoric (situational) and endophoric (textual) reference that M. A. K. Halliday and Ruqaiya Hasan (1976) discuss in *Cohesion in English.* Halliday and Hasan emphasize that the pronouns "you" and "we" are typically exophoric, occurring in specific rhetorical situations that are heavily context dependent and in turn "point" toward certain social and cultural understandings. Clearly, this is the case with the syllabi in question, which are understandable only within the context of the class, instructor, institution, and more broadly within a culture that thinks about composition studies in certain ways.

In terms of understanding that situation, Halliday and Hasan (1976) suggest that "a high degree of exophoric reference" is one characteristic of the language of "the children's peer group" and go on to make a connection to Basil Bernstein's (1964) "restricted code," a method of communication heavily dependent on the context of the situation. Halliday and Hasan help explain how, as Bawarshi suggests, the use of "you" coupled with "we" acts as a hailing gesture that interpellates student subjects who are drawn into the collective "we" (Bawarshi 2003) and, by extension, into a kind of restricted code. Under Bawarshi's analysis, the nature of that relationship is coercive on the part of the teacher, who tries to make it seem consensual: "The 'we' construction tries to minimize the teacher's power implicit in the 'you' construction by making it appear as though the students are more than merely passive recipients of the teacher's dictates" (123). The work of both Althusser and Bernstein takes that a step further, suggesting that the pronouns work as a kind of infantilizing gesture that reveals the real dynamic between the "you and we": the instructor's gesture toward an ostensibly democratizing "we" actually drawing upon situational knowledge that constructs students, through the syllabus, as dependent parts of a hierarchical relationship.

In addition to this deictic aspect of these personal pronouns, Halliday and Hasan help show how the pronoun reference analyzed by Bawarshi becomes more complicated still: pronouns that are typically exophoric—pointing to an outward reality—often become anaphoric—referring to the previous part of a text—in many varieties of written language. The composition syllabus, which is at heart exophoric because of the constant juxtaposition of "you" and "we" (and, by extension, "I") (see below) and their reference to an external reality, may become anaphoric, particularly when those pronouns refer to an institutional rule or policy that the instructor is quoting. Here, the role of the pronouns shifts so that the relationship between the instructor ("I" or "we") and students ("you") becomes a textual reference, which makes the authority of the syllabus writer easier to maintain. Thus, the syllabus essentially functions in a dialectic relationship between exophoric and anaphoric reference, and this suggests one way the instructor is able to maintain the balance she must achieve between what Bawarshi calls "community and complicity" (123). The syllabus writer makes both an inclusive and distancing gesture and, through the use of pronouns, is able to build solidarity. Even though Bawarshi is correct in asserting that there is a tension in this kind of passive-aggressive interpellation, his analysis could draw upon style as a tool that would significantly improve its persuasive appeal by showing why the pronouns function in this manner.

Bawarshi indicates the dynamic nature of genre in composition studies when he contends that the syllabus "is not merely informative; it is also, as all genres are, a site of action that produces subjects who desire to act in certain ideological and discursive ways" (125). In constructing the syllabus as genre, Bawarshi suggests that its writers use the pronouns "you" and "we" in a way that "positions students and teachers within situated subjectivities and relations" (121). While intimating that the use of pronouns is important in creating a kind of subjectivity in the composition syllabus, he relies on the interplay of "you" and "we" without pointing out the importance of "we" as a complicated pronoun connected to an underlying "I." However, French philosopher Emile Benveniste (1971), a contemporary of Althusser's, articulates the importance of the intricate connection between the use of "we" or "I" and "you" when he writes:

> In "we" it is always "I" which predominates since there cannot be "we" except by starting with "I," and this "I" dominates the "non-I" element by means of its transcendent quality. *The presence of "I" is constitutive of "we."* (202; emphasis added)

While Bawarshi suggests that the "we" is used by the instructor to interpellate student subjects ("you"), Benveniste's analysis of pronouns (which Bawarshi does *not* use) offers a more reciprocal view of this subjectivity. By looking more broadly than Bawarshi does at the "I" behind the "we," Benveniste helps us argue that the dichotomy of "I" and "you" is imperative in order for the subjectivity of the teacher to exist:

> Consciousness of self is only possible if it is experienced by contrast. I use *I* only when I am speaking to someone who will be a *you* in my address. It is this condition of dialogue that is constitutive of person, for it implies that reciprocally *I* becomes *you* in the address of the one who in his turn designates himself *I*. Here we see a principle whose consequences are to spread out in all directions. Language

> is possible only because each speaker sets himself up as a subject by referring to himself as *I* in his discourse. Because of this, *I* posits another person, the one who, being, as he is, completely exterior to "me," becomes my echo to whom I say *you* and who says *you* to me. (224–25)

Benveniste's analysis, which is similar to Mikhail Bakhtin's (1981) concepts of "svoj" (one's own voice) and "čužoj" (the voice of another) (423), adds a great deal to the discussion of the purpose of the genre of the syllabus because Benveniste makes clear that the writer (the instructor) as "I" (sometimes, as Bawarshi points out, in the form of "we") is constituted through his or her own discourse. Thus, the dialectic between the "I" or "we" and the "you" is an important part of the identity of both, but does not necessarily entail an equal relationship. As Benveniste states, "This polarity does not mean either equality or symmetry: 'ego' always has a position of transcendence with regard to you" (Benveniste 1971, 225). In the syllabi Bawarshi analyzes, there is evidence of the same unsettling inequality, even in the use of "we" to include the instructor in the learning enterprise.

Even in the face of the inequality inherent in this dialectic, however, Benveniste points out that there is also an unusual sense of reciprocity. He writes that "neither of the terms can be conceived of without the other. They are complementary . . . and, at the same time, they are reversible" (225). This contention is quite provocative, yet Bawarshi's construction of the syllabus as genre does not account for the full stylistic potential it affords. Admittedly, Bawarshi (2003) does suggest that the pronouns can be complementary on one level when he writes that the "interchange between 'you' and 'we' on the pronoun level reflects a larger tension many teachers face when writing a syllabus: between establishing solidarity with students and demarcating lines of authority" (122). However, Bawarshi does not imagine a scenario in which the roles are reversible. If, for example, the syllabus were to refer to the part of the course where students evaluate the instructor, or to students assuming the role of teacher for a peer-writing workshop, the full import of the reversibility of pronouns could be realized. Benveniste invites us to acknowledge the ambivalent relationship between power and shared authority in the syllabus genre. The complicated relationship of the pronouns gives students who are otherwise "interpellated" a kind of agency and power that Bawarshi attributes only to the teacher. Through the syllabus, students are constructed as writers themselves. When they write, they become the "I." While Bawarshi points to pronoun (and other stylistic) relationships in promising ways, his analysis does not fully recognize the potential ways in which the instructor/student interactions might change as they are constructed through language.

RHETORICAL ANALYSIS

The study of style has not only moved into genre studies, but into one of the main sites that composition claims as part of its disciplinary identity: rhetorical analysis. Jeanne Fahnestock and Marie Secor (2002) write that "rhetorical analysis, whether of a written or a spoken text, must always factor into account the speaker, audience, context, and 'moment' of a text as explanatory principles for the linguistic and strategic choices identified" (178). In identifying "linguistic and strategic choices," the authors raise key words in the study of style. The idea of choice has always been crucial to style, and many aspects of stylistic analysis are seen as linguistic as well as rhetorical. While acknowledging a historical tradition of style, however, the authors end by incorporating it as simply a small part of "rhetorical analysis." Thus, when viewed in terms of Lauer's concept of the diaspora, rhetorical analysis becomes a site of dispersion that includes various aspects of stylistic analysis, such as vocabulary, syntax, and the classical tropes and schemes. The authors' appropriation of style as rhetoric raises an important question: If the method used is stylistic analysis, is there a greater advantage in calling it by that name?

I argue that the answer is "yes," and as an example I cite a "rhetorical analysis" by Fahnestock and Secor in which they examine a controversy over Alan Sokal's postmodern "farce" that is the subject of an editorial by Fish (1996) for the *New York Times.* Sokal (1996a), a physicist at New York University, submitted a postmodern critique of quantum mechanics that was subsequently accepted and published by the editors of the journal *Social Text.* Afterward, in an article in *Lingua Franca,* Sokal (1996b) claimed that his *Social Text* article was a parody and was published with factual errors that the editors, who did not follow the standard practice of sending the piece out for scholarly review, had not caught. Fish, then a professor of law and literature at Duke University, and editor of Duke University Press, which publishes *Social Text,* wrote about the hoax on the op-ed pages of the *Times* and, as Fahnestock and Secor (2002) describe it, "helped to turn Sokal's parody into an academic *cause celebre*" (185). Fish's opinion piece serves as the subject of Fahnestock and Secor's rhetorical analysis. They begin by analyzing Fish's use of register, voice, and colloquial terms:

> Consider first how Fish's level or register shifting contributes to his distinctive voice. For example, he mixes vocabulary from a formal, scholarly register with informal or colloquial terms: "Distinguishing fact from fiction is surely the business of science, but the means of doing so are not perspicuous in nature—for if they were, there would be no work to be done." The term "business" as used here and the phrases "work to be done" and "fact from fiction" are less formal. More formal—that is, less conversational—are the choices "surely" and "the means of doing so." (191)

The analysis of Fish's text, which Fahnestock and Secor place under the subheading of "appeals to ethos," continues as the authors look carefully at some of Fish's use of vocabulary and shifts in register:

> But the most striking word choice in the sentence, "perspicuous," is an unusual if not arcane usage. Fish apparently uses this word in the sense of "clear" or "easy to understand," but because "perspicuous" and its noun form "perspicuity" are usually applied to language

> (indeed, perspicuity is one of the four virtues of style in rhetoric), the application to "nature" is a self-conscious stretch. The word itself suggests the notion of nature as a text to be read with interpretive difference, a notion that comes from the disciplinary camp of sociologists of science. Notice too the register shifts within the sentence, from low at the beginning and end to high in the middle: The overall impression is of accessibility, but there is a marked formality amidst the casual. Fish's choices seem to say, "I can communicate on your level, but I'm doing so from above." (191–92)

While the authors clearly identify the importance of style in mentioning (parenthetically) that Fish's use of "perspicuity" alludes to a virtue of style, they do not acknowledge that their *entire* analysis is essentially a stylistic analysis. Their interest in register (formal vs. informal or colloquial), voice, vocabulary, diction (word choice), syntax, and more is, by definition, stylistic, and that analysis is crucial to uncovering the underlying meaning and intention of the author. If the Fahnestock and Secor analysis is clearly stylistic, why is it important to identify it specifically as style instead of more generally as rhetoric, which is what the authors call it? I argue that by labeling their analysis "style," the authors would bring to bear a great deal of knowledge about style onto another tradition. This suggests that the rhetorical tradition includes a rich stylistic component with a plethora of analytical tools that are not being fully exploited here. Style is a key ingredient in creating the underlying meaning that Fish intends and, by being aware of it, readers could uncover other levels of meaning tied to stylistic analysis.

While style looks closely at sentences and the meanings inherent in them, it makes sense only in relation to broader patterns of discourse and thus has an inextricable connection to arrangement and form. Secor and Fahenstock allude to many rhetorical traditions in their article, yet they do not show this dynamic interplay among style and other canons of the rhetorical tradition. In her article "Kairotic Encounters," Debra Hawhee (2002) writes:

> When rhetoric emerges from encounters, invention is practiced on many levels: in the unexpected syncopations that occur under the traditional rubric of "style"; in the strategic piecing together of discourse (also called "arrangement"); in the bodily and "surface" movements sometimes called "delivery"; and in the configurations of experiential "memory." (33)

In finding many similarities between what they call discourse analysis (involving language resources at the word and sentence level) and rhetorical analysis (which they say implies broader patterns and forms of discourse), Fahnestock and Secor (2002) acknowledge that "different lenses always produce different visions and the more lenses and visions, the better" (195). What the authors do not acknowledge, however, is the presence of style and the debt that their distinction between discourse and rhetorical analysis owes to style. While Fahenstock and Secor discuss the tradition of style—and elaborate at some length about the nature of its contributions to rhetoric—they seem to see it primarily as a historical phenomenon, and not one currently part of the lexicon of rhetoric. Admittedly, the authors go on to describe traditional attributes of style, such as register, rhetorical schemes and tropes, and lexical field, yet in their failure to describe style's current relevance to their analysis, they relegate stylistic resources to the by-product of a previous era. In their "rhetorical analysis" of the Sokal text, however, it is clear that they have broadly appropriated the tools of stylistic analysis, generally without acknowledging them as stylistic. This strategy fails to acknowledge that what the authors are performing in the name of rhetorical analysis involves, in large part, an analysis of style.

PERSONAL WRITING

Another example of the migration of style into composition's diaspora is the field's recent interest in memoir, creative nonfiction, and autobiography, which cuts across many disciplines in a meta-narrative of local concerns. In the field of composition, several special issues of *College English* (see Hesse 2003;

Hindman 2001, 2003) have been devoted to that study: one in creative nonfiction and two on the personal in academic writing, as well as individual articles on the genre of scholarly memoir in various academic publications. In an edited collection on "the personal," *Personal Effects: The Social Character of Scholarly Writing*, editors David Bleich and Deborah Holdstein (2001) write, "To one degree or another, scholarly authors' lived experiences are already part of the different subject matters in the humanities" (2). Though this interest can be viewed in a number of ways, I suggest that one of its features is an interest in register as related to stylistic choices about vocabulary, the use of pronouns to form a persona, and experiments with syntax, tense, and form that focus on the style of these various genres as experimentation and play. As is true with other aspects of the stylistic migration I have been discussing, however, the renewed interest in these genres ignores a potentially useful discussion of style. James Kinneavy (1971) described some of these useful aims of style, including the style of expressive discourse, in his work *A Theory of Discourse.*

Jane Hindman (2001) has used a blending of academic and nonacademic styles, registers, vocabulary, and typography to point to opposing views of authorizing experience in discourse. In her argument for the use of the personal in academic discourse, Hindman weaves together various aspects of her own personae. In her innovative use of various levels of discourse, however, Hindman does not ever characterize any element of her work as stylistic or allude to style in any way. In "Making Writing Matter: Using 'the Personal' to Recover[y] an Essential[ist] Tension in Academic Discourse," Hindman (2001) weaves stylistic experience as follows:

> Many, however, object—sometimes strenuously—to proposals that academics use "the personal" as a way to renounce mastery and share a common discourse. . . . I would additionally define this tension as the conflict between opposing conceptions of an expressivist, autobiographical self whose autonomy creates coherence out

> of inchoate experience and a socially constructed self who is always already constrained by the conventions of discourse.
>
> *No, no, no. This is not the way to make things clear: I'm already fogging up the issue with jargon like "agency" and "subject[ivitie]s" and critical affirmation." And this way that I'm thinking I'm so clever by using "matter" to mean something it doesn't really mean: what's up with that? I can't get what I'm talking about any more. What is my point here? I'm so concerned with getting in the right sources that I can't get in what I want to say. Can't I keep this simple? Start over.*
>
> My name's JaneE and I'm an alcoholic. My sobriety date is January 1, 1987. I'm glad to be here today. As I understand the topic, the issue we're discussing is what makes someone "really" an alcoholic. Is it the word, the label, or is it something in her? How can you tell the difference? (89–90)

In Hindman's autobiographical essay, it is clear that with each persona she adopts, the writer uses a different register or level of language appropriate for the occasion. In trying to give each "voice" or persona a different but equal authority, Hindman experiments with stylistic variation, suggesting that the informal quality of inner speech (see Vygotsky 1997) can be just as powerful in revealing the questions we ask ourselves as more formal academic prose. In this sense, the style (e.g., the variation in vocabulary, syntax, register, and so forth) of each separate persona has meaning in itself. Take, for example, the contrast between the style of the first and third paragraphs. The first paragraph, heavily indebted to the genre of academic discourse, draws on a particular vocabulary as well as a somewhat complicated syntax. Thus, for example, when Hindman (2001) writes that there is tension in "the conflict between opposing conceptions of an expressivist, autobiographical self whose autonomy creates coherence out of inchoate experience and a socially constructed self who is always already constrained by the conventions of discourse" (106), she clearly draws upon the language of the discipline ("expressivist," "socially constructed") and a meta-discourse of poststructuralist expressions that characterize the conflicts in language in a certain way ("always already constrained," "inchoate experience," and "constrained by the conventions of discourse"). Through vocabulary, she in turn adopts a register (formal, "academic," intellectual) that mimics the jargon of the field.

When regarded alone, the nature of this academic discourse does not seem unusual. However, when Hindman juxtaposes the academic discourse—albeit on the topic of "the personal"—with a far less formal third paragraph related to the genre of the confession, the contrast is striking. Most readers, even those unfamiliar with formal academic discourse, will be familiar with the confessional genre so prevalent in 12-step or personal improvement programs that have become cultural commonplaces. In the latter discourse, Hindman embraces the confessional style through the use of the pronoun "I" and the use of the formulaic confession ("My name's JaneE and I'm an alcoholic"). At the same time, however, Hindman, through stylistic means, questions the "simplicity" of the simple sentences and uncomplicated vocabulary of the confession. By superimposing upon the confessional genre an "academic style" ("As I understand the topic, the issue we're discussing is what makes someone 'really' an alcoholic. Is it the word, the label, or is it something in her?"), she challenges the separation between these two supposedly distinct genres.

Hindman's blurring of styles and genres happens again when she questions self-reflexively the very academic "moves" she is making, taking on the persona of the self-doubting writer *("No, no, no. This is not the way to make things clear: I'm already fogging up the issue with jargon like "agency" and "subject[ivitie]s" and "critical affirmation")* (Hindman 2001, 90). As with the other personae she adopts, Hindman uses typography, a stylistic feature that goes beyond sentences, to indicate the multiperspectival nature of her discourse. What's more, the juxtaposition of the self-reflexive vocabulary ("fogging up," "no, no, no") with the words she is constantly questioning (e.g., "agency" and "subject[ivitie]s") reveals the importance of style in constructing discourse. Her desire to show the importance of the "personal" is made much greater by the blending of styles in creating her own academic discourse. The various uses of voice, register, vocabulary, and tone suggests an interest in style as play, as experimentation that the author never identifies explicitly as style but clearly embodies throughout her writing.

Autobiography and memoir implicate the study of style in composition in other important ways. Style reaches across the boundaries of genre to imbue language with a consciousness of gender, class, and ethnicity. Margaret K. Willard-Traub (2003) alludes to this tendency in her article "Rhetorics of Gender and Ethnicity in Scholarly Memoir," where she writes:

> Memoirs and autobiographically inflected texts . . . strongly reject language as a "transparent medium for" simply holding or conveying meaning, especially meaning related to such aspects of identity as ethnicity, gender, and class. Instead, these texts . . . conceive of language as a "material constituent in" the social relations that encourage particular understandings of identity within and across particular communities. (512)

Scholarship in rhetoric and composition has been filled with scholarly memoir that uses variation in style to look *at* (rather than *through*) language itself (Lanham 1974) as a source of meaning and identity. In works such as Keith Gilyard's *Voices of the Self* (1990), Victor Villanueva's *Bootstraps* (1993), and Mike Rose's *Lives on the Boundary* (1989), the authors explore different writing styles that capture the often conflicting nature of their personal and professional identities. Indeed, this is not reserved exclusively for academics, but incorporates everything from political memoir—the instances of former president Bill Clinton, his wife Hillary Rodham Clinton, and whistle blower Richard Clark come to mind—to personal memoirs by American expatriate David Sedaris, writer Joan Didion, and *Meet the Press* moderator Tim Russert. Clearly, some of the movement into memoir has been controversial. For instance, in his biographical memoir of Ronald Reagan, *Dutch: A Memoir of Ronald Reagan*, Edmund Morris (1999) decides to relate the period of time before he met Reagan (and for which he had no personal memory) by creating a persona. Morris makes a stylistic choice to form a persona through which he conveys specific information about the late president's life. Given the outcry that accompanied this decision, it is clear that the genre of personal writing is popular—and controversial—outside the academy.

In their interest in this type of writing, composition scholars also look across disciplines to find ways in which style is connected to larger issues. Willard-Traub (2003), for example, uses examples from various disciplines to make the point that the personal and professional are connected to identity, often through what she says is "the language of loss." While she does not mention style specifically, Willard-Traub's work implicates style in many crucial ways. For example, she writes:

> Scholars across the disciplines such as Ruth Behar in anthropology, Patricia Williams in law, Alice Kaplan in French studies, Shirley Geok-lin Lim in English, among others, have demonstrated in their scholarly work, much of which draws on examples from personal experience, how academic and professional languages, for example, are not separable from the behaviors of historically real human groups that have functioned to place women, people of color, and the poor in subordinate positions both outside and within the academy. (513)

While Willard-Traub's claim at first seems simply to explore the way in which personal and professional languages are connected to social patterns or behaviors, her specific analysis of this interconnection is, at heart, a function of style. Thus, for example, when Willard-Traub looks to Ruth Behar in the field of anthropology, she cites the latter's essay, "Writing in My Father's Name" (Behar 1995), to draw attention to a style she calls "shadow biography" as well as to larger issues of form and discourse. According to Traub, Behar (1993) achieves part of her effect by restructuring her essay through a series of diary entries that examine her family's reaction to her book *Translated Woman: Crossing the Border with Esperanza's Story* (1993), the ethnography of a Mexican peddler woman. At one point, Traub cites the instance of Behar's interpellation into the academic community after receiving both tenure and a MacArthur fellowship. Behar (1993) writes:

> I was now lost in a different wilderness, the wilderness of success in the university system, success I myself had striven for. After being the woman who couldn't translate herself, I had suddenly become the woman who translated herself too well. And in the midst of it all, I was planning to turn the tales of a Mexican street peddler into a book that would be read within the very same academy that had toyed with my intimate sense of identity and then, with even less compunction, bought me out. Fresh from the horror of being a translated woman, I would now turn around and translate another woman for consumption on this side of the border. (335)

Willard-Traub (2003) interprets Behar's writing as an example of the "institutional rhetoric" in which Behar herself is complicit, an example, according to Willard-Traub, that works by "'translating' individuals into 'others' for particular audiences and purposes." In a rather prescient analysis, Willard-Traub adds that "*in the same moment,* Behar's reflection also blurs the dividing line between herself and Esperanza by acknowledging that both are vulnerable . . . to having their lived experiences and identities rewritten in ways outside of their control" (515; emphasis original).

Even though Willard-Traub's analysis reveals the way in which Behar and Esperanza's identities can become blurred or confused, where the subject becomes both the subjected and the agent of subjugation, her negotiation of this border territory would be enriched through stylistic analysis. In particular, I argue that the use of style is what reveals how the border becomes blurred—and thus illuminates the consequences of that blurring. That blurring occurs through Behar's own skilful use of rhetorical schemes and tropes. The metaphor of translation, to begin with, itself suggests a certain blurring of boundaries between language, nationality, and idiom: it allows the translator to become both interpreter and interpreted, her own "translation" refracted through the lens of the "translated's" subjectivity. Behar shows the nature of these double boundaries through the use of *anadiplosis*, or the repetition of the last word of one clause at the beginning of the following clause (Corbett 1971, 475). For example, she writes, "wilderness, the wilderness," "success in the university system, success" and then follows that up by weaving in the scheme of antithesis: "After being *the woman who couldn't translate herself*, I had suddenly become *the woman who translated herself too well*," an idea she continues with another example: "from the horror of being a translated woman" and "translate another woman" (Behar 1993, 335; emphasis added). By using these rhetorical schemes, mediated through the trope of metaphor, Behar mirrors syntactically—and stylistically—the reciprocal effect of her actions. The repetition of words has the effect of an antiphonal choir, the acted upon and the acting of language.

In addition to Behar, Willard-Traub also mentions Asian writer Shirley Geok-lin Lim (1996) who, in *Among the White Moon Faces*, shows how the form of autobiographical writing becomes a meta-narrative about the loss of place and identity in both personal and professional homelands. Geok-lin writes:

> The dominant imprint I have carried with me since birth was of a Malaysian homeland. It has been an imperative for me to make sense of these birthmarks; they compose the hieroglyphs of my body's senses. We tell stories to bind us to a spot, and often the stories that make us cry knot the thickest ropes. (231)

Later, Lim writes about the displacement she feels as she moves around within the United States, her new home:

> To give up the struggle for a memorialized homeland may be the most forgiving act I can do. Everywhere I have lived in the United States—Boston, Brooklyn, Westchester—I felt an absence of place,

myself absent in America. Absence was the story my mother taught me, that being the story of her migrant people, the Malacca peranakans. But perhaps she was also teaching me that home is the place where our stories are told. Had I more time to talk to Mother, perhaps I could have learned to forgive, listening to her stories. In California, I am beginning to write stories about America, as well as about Malaysia. Listening, and telling my own stories, I am moving home. (231–32)

What remains under the surface in this powerful narrative is the importance of style. While Lim's conflict between place and displacement may be clear, it is more powerful when some of the elements of style are used to reveal how she achieves this effect. For example, Lim's use of occasional periodic sentences to delay the impact of her ideas is a function of style that helps to enact the power and emotion of her displacement and reacculturation. She writes, "To give up the struggle for a memorialized homeland *may be the most forgiving act I can do,*" and then, "Listening, and telling my stories, *I am moving home*" (emphasis added). In both instances, delaying the resolution of the sentence until the end works to extend the pain of her displacement and furthers the anticipation of its resolution. In addition, Lim uses the rhetorical scheme of *polyptoton,* or the repetition of words derived from the same root, to accentuate the feeling of loss, in this case, the various forms of the word "absence/absent." Thus, for instance, she writes, "I felt an absence of place, myself absent in America. Absence was the story my mother taught me" (Lim 1996, 231).

Lim also effectively combines two other rhetorical schemes to achieve her purposes: *asyndeton* and *parenthesis.* In her sentence, "Everywhere I have lived in the United States—Boston, Brooklyn, Westchester—I felt an absence of place, myself absent in America," the parenthesis achieved through the use of dashes—Boston, Brooklyn, Westchester—juxtaposes in an abrupt form locations that are easily recognizable for Americans with the lack of recognition they hold for Lim. In addition, Lim's use of parenthesis is accompanied by the use, in the same sentence, of asyndeton, the "deliberate omission of conjunctions between a series of related clauses" (Corbett 1971, 469). The effect of asyndeton (Boston, Brooklyn, Westchester), especially when it is used in conjunction with parenthesis, is to present the cities in a staccato effect, the one-two-three punch of words that are simply names in a list rather than attached to personal—or cultural—memory. The stylistic effect is to show how the cities themselves are alienated from Lim, not just Lim from them. While there are other stylistic schemes at work here, these few examples demonstrate how important style is to achieving the overall effect of Lim's feeling of being both absent and present, in America and Malaysia, a feeling that is not alleviated until she realizes the importance of telling her own stories. The point is that the stylistic features, which exist on an implicit plane, are powerful when made explicit: they become an important part of the overall effect, meaning, emotion, and consensus the author is trying to achieve. The interest in the genre of personal writing, therefore, is imbued with the study of style, even though it is not acknowledged or recognized in that way.

One question that must still be answered is to what extent style can be construed as going beyond sentences (see Roen 1996). In other words, in addition to stylistic features that are primarily syntactic, how much does the form of the genre itself affect the way that style has dispersed into the diaspora? In Hindman's (2001) essay, for example, the difference in typography reflects the changing personae she adopts. To what degree is this change in the form of the essay—the congruence of identity and form—a stylistic feature, or as Duane Roen asks, how does it reflect a feature of discourse at a broader level of concern (193)? The dispersion of style into personal writing suggests that style, while manifested locally in sentences, has important impacts on the broader form of discourse. It seems that the attention to memoir, autobiography, and creative nonfiction in composition is focused primarily at that broader level. What is clear, however, is that those features of the broader form of discourse—for example, Hindman's distinctive typography, or Behar's use of journal entries—become most important through the stylistic features enacted in sentences. Therefore, while it may be tempting to try to make a pronouncement about the migration of style into broader forms of discourse—the idea of arrangement or, perhaps, that of genre—it seems that the real dispersion, and its importance, must concomitantly be viewed at the level of the sentence.

THEORIES OF RACE, CLASS, GENDER, AND CULTURAL DIFFERENCE

One of the most surprising areas into which style has moved is theories of race, class, gender, and cultural difference in composition. Since the social "turn" in composition, and even in light of CCCC's declaration of "Students' Right to Their Own Language" (Committee on CCCC Language 1974), the field has turned forcefully toward these theories within which there has been an emphasis on style in ways often not evident. One way this is manifested is in the notion of a "personal" style: the idea that language is most clearly evident in the way it is taken up by each person; the principle of variation; and, ultimately, the concept of diversity. The notion of variation is important in the definition and idea of style. It suggests that style is composed of variation from a norm and it is the juxtaposition of variation and normalization that produces the style. Clearly, this view has been important in many aspects of cultural studies.

Style has been important in theories of social class that have become increasingly significant in composition in recent years. Those who embody the tensions of trying to value their background, roots, and socioeconomic status often adopt a style appropriate to communicating their struggle. This conflict is evident in Laurel Johnson Black's (1995) essay, "Stupid Rich Bastards," in which she discusses the difficulty of growing up in a working-class family, a way of life in which "bodily functions, secretions, garbage, crimes and delinquency, who got away with what were as much a part of our language as they were of our lives" (15). In positing another vocabulary, a register as a way of life, Black is essentially advancing an argument about social class through stylistic choices. Through the study of style, we see how she achieves this balance, articulating her angry vision as she is pulled between two worlds:

> At some point in my life, when I was very young, it had been decided that I would be the one who went to college, who earned a lot of money, who pulled my family away from the edge of the pit, and who gave the stupid rich bastards what they had coming to them. I would speak like them but wouldn't be one of them. I would move among them, would spy on them, learn their ways, and explain them to my own people—a guerrilla fighter for the poor. My father had visions of litigation dancing in his head, his daughter in a suit, verbally slapping the hell out of some rich asshole in a courtroom. (17)

Through the use of the passive voice ("it had been decided that I"), Black (1995) erases her own agency so that she becomes simply a force of the working class from which she hails. She shows the conflict in even greater detail through the repetition of the pronoun "who" ("I would be the one *who* went to college, *who* earned a lot of money, *who* pulled my family away from the edge of the pit, and *who* gave the stupid rich bastards what they had coming to them") (17; emphasis added); each successive repetition of the relative pronoun both includes her as part of the class yet distances her from the person she actually is—and the person she is becoming. She also distances herself from the class she is joining by use of the conditional tense, "would" (i.e., "I *would* speak like them but *wouldn't* be one of them. I *would* move among them, *would* spy on them") (17; emphasis added). The use of the conditional makes her simply a player in the overall actions of the working class with which she so closely identifies herself. These stylistic techniques allow Black to use the language of the working class, to adopt its vocabulary without fully embracing it. Thus, the effect is to make the use of her language somehow disembodied. Therefore, when she writes about the "stupid rich bastards" and "verbally slapping the hell out of some rich asshole," the reader is left with a curious effect: words that seem to be representative of the working class, but that seem distant—perhaps appropriately—for a woman who has entered a middle-class existence. This tension, between working and middle classes, between solidarity with her class and the fact of having left it, appears prominently in her stylistic moves.

In *Traces of a Stream: Literacy and Social Change among African American Women*, Jacqueline Jones Royster (2000) focuses on style in analyzing the literacy practices of some of the early American women she studies. In looking at the style of essayist/poet/novelist Alice Walker, Royster writes:

> In terms of style, Walker does not always remain within conventional boundaries of exposition and argumentation. She weaves in and out of these modes—at will, as a master storyteller might do—and operates as if there were indeed a fluid space in which both autonomous and non-autonomous rhetorical choices can be selected. Sometimes she uses narration, description, dialogue, poetry, and powerful images, not just as interest-generating opening devices but as elaboration, as evidence for assertions that appeal to readers in terms of logos, pathos, and ethos. Further, she consistently pays attention to the triadic relationships between herself, her audience, and the subject matter, referencing her personal vision and experiences and the context in which she exists. (40)

Clearly, the very fact that Royster attributes these characteristics of Walker's writing to style is evidence of style having migrated in composition into explorations of race and gender. Royster's observations include Walker's use of "the voices of others" (40). Part of Royster's discussion of style, however, is primarily one of genre: argumentation, the genre of storytelling, and so forth. I submit that the actual language and techniques of stylistic analysis might lead Royster to some unexpected conclusions about the connection between literacy and social action.

Royster takes important steps in stylistic analysis when she quotes the following passage from an Alice Walker (1983) essay on Zora Neale Hurston:

> Without money of one's own in a capitalist society, there is no such thing as independence. This is one of the clearest lessons of Zora's life, and why I consider the telling of her life "a cautionary tale." We must learn from it what we can. . . . Without money, an illness, even a simple one, can undermine the will. Without money, getting into a hospital is problematic and getting out without money to pay for the treatment is nearly impossible. Without money, one becomes dependent on other people, who are likely to be—even in their kindness—erratic in their support and despotic in their expectations of return. Zora was forced to rely, like Tennessee Williams's Blanche, "on the kindness of strangers." Can anything be more dangerous, if the strangers are forever in control? Zora, who worked so hard, was never able to make a living from her work. (90)

In her analysis, Royster refers to Walker's use of a rhetorical scheme that Edward P. J. Corbett (1971) calls *anaphora* ("repetition of the same word or group of words at the beginnings of successive clauses") (472) in the phrase "without money," as well as in the rhetorical question (i.e., "Can anything be more dangerous?"), both of which are promising stylistic areas. In a more formal stylistic analysis, Royster might also observe how Walker uses this repetition to achieve a strong emotional effect precisely because it illustrates the futility of what Hurston tries to accomplish. The greatness of her accomplishment stands in direct contrast to her impoverishment. Thus, with the use of anaphora—and the result that Hurston, Blanche Dubois-like, had to rely on the "kindness of strangers"—the subsequent posing of a rhetorical question, "Can anything be more dangerous, if the strangers are forever in control?" has the typical effect of asking a question in order to assert something obliquely rather than eliciting an answer. While this is often the province of impassioned speeches, Walker's use of the rhetorical question in this instance serves to elicit a certain response from the audience and to make the suggestion much more powerfully than if she had made the statement directly.

Given the purpose of Royster's work, the stylistic practices could also show the plight of poverty among African-American women and allude to Walker's point that it served to delay or deny greatness among African-American women. These results are achieved through style, and Royster is showing how style is being used effectively by Walker. Royster's contribution to the diaspora is therefore laudable. Her work is a promising step toward integrating stylistic analysis into a site of the diaspora that holds great interest for the field.

IMPLICATIONS

The idea that the study of style has not disappeared from the field of composition completely but has migrated into other areas offers several opportunities for the field. The idea of the diaspora, brilliant in conception, is nonetheless troubling if it is thought of as a "forced" migration. Yet, evidence suggests that with respect to style, for composition scholars the diaspora represents more a state of self-imposed exile than a forced flight. Regardless of the popular cultural forces that may have led to a flight from stylistic study in composition, there is really no reason for the field to consider the expulsion forced. If that is the case, the field needs to acknowledge the examples of stylistic study found in many areas in which that work has diffused. Several are mentioned here; many others exist.

While it would be useful to students to have access to these stylistic resources as they develop as writers, I argue that it would be equally beneficial to composition scholars. My analysis has attempted to show that scholars with excellent rhetorical skills are not exploiting the full range of stylistic—and thus analytical—options that would allow a more complete understanding of textual objects. Stylistic analysis includes a rich tradition of practices and resources that are available for writers to use, and their neglect, I contend, leaves important gaps in any written work. While the stylistic work that currently exists in diffused areas may hint at some of the possibilities, an analysis that exploits the resources of style explicitly would have a greater command of the uses of language in different contexts. If it is true that style, like invention, has not only migrated but "entered, settled, and shaped many other areas of theory and practice in rhetoric and composition" (Lauer 2002, 2), then it seems important for the field to acknowledge an important source of its work. It will require a change in attitude, however, for the field to embrace the study of style and, in redeploying it in useful ways, effectively redefine it for the field. The diaspora of composition studies offers an ideal site for the discipline to begin that change.[2]

5

STYLE AND THE PUBLIC INTELLECTUAL

Rethinking Composition in the Public Sphere

In 2005, contributors to the Writing Program Administration Listserv (WPA-L) responded angrily when Stanley Fish, in a *New York Times* op-ed piece, derided decades of composition scholarship by stating that "content is a lure and a delusion and should be banished from the classroom." In its place, Fish advocates "form," his term for the grammar he asks students to use as they construct a new language. In his column, "Devoid of Content," the renowned literary scholar laments the emphasis on content in composition courses because of what he argues is the field's mistaken belief that "if you chew over big ideas long enough, the ability to write about them will (mysteriously) follow" (Fish 2005). He thus exorcises intellectual concepts, anthologized readings, controversy, and everything else except "how prepositions or participles or relative pronouns function." While compositionists' opposition to Fish's critique of "so-called courses in writing" is to be expected—in a letter to the *Times,* Deborah Brandt (2005) states that "what Stanley Fish teaches isn't writing"—their reaction is surprising in one respect: Fish (2002) had made almost the same claim three years earlier in the *Chronicle of Higher Education,* where he writes that content, useful *initially* to illustrate syntactical or rhetorical points, should then be "avoided like the plague." If Fish is merely rehashing an old argument, what accounts for the outcry over his later column only? On the WPA list, one contributor suggested that the problem was its public circulation: "Because it went to *The New York Times,* it circumvents the entire academic community and speaks directly to an audience that already believes that academics don't know what they are doing, especially when it comes to writing" (Galin 2005).

Unfortunately, Fish's commentary on the discipline is far from an isolated occurrence. In what seems at first to be nothing more than a relatively short *New Yorker* book review of a "throwback" style guide for college students, former CUNY English professor Louis Menand (2000), now at Harvard, ends up defining rhetoric and composition for readers—and his account is anything but flattering. Menand's review of literature professor David R. Williams's (2000) how-to text, *Sin Boldly! Dr. Dave's Guide to Writing College Papers* is, simply put, a critique of composition studies, and what is particularly distressing is the way in which the staff writer for the *New Yorker* uses the piece to introduce the field in ways that are reductive, outdated, and unsupported by disciplinary scholarship. Take, for example, this early paragraph in Menand's article, "Comp Time: Is College Too Late to Learn How to Write?":

> Rhet Comp specialists have their own nomenclature: they talk about things like "sentence boundaries," and they design instructional units around concepts like "Division and Classification" and "Definition and Process." These are trained discipline professionals. They understand writing for what it is, a technology, and they have the patience and expertise to take on the combination of psychotherapy and social work that teaching people how to write basically boils down to. (Menand 2000, 92)

Even though Robert Connors countered the assumption that composition uses a modal (e.g., "division and classification") and, by extension, current-traditional, approach to writing instruction in an award-winning essay published in 1981, Menand nonetheless makes that implicit claim with impunity on the pages of the *New Yorker*—not to mention reducing writing, without complicating the notion, to merely "a technology" (see Ong 1982, 81–83). The staff writer then goes on to devalue the writing process: "Students are often told, for example, to write many drafts. . . . Here is a scandalous thing to say, but it's true: you are reading the first draft of this review" (94). In this statement, Menand contradicts a common practice—revision—that not only compositionists, but most professional writers, generally take as a given. He further misses the point of revision when he asks, "Would you tell a builder to get the skyscraper up any way he or she could, and then go back and start working on the foundations?" (93), thereby eschewing the more fitting comparison of a writer to an architect who may produce a number of preliminary designs before deciding on a "final" one that might be subject to additional changes. Menand's somewhat flippant charge that writing instruction combines "psychotherapy and social work" is exacerbated when he equates practices like free writing ("the whole 'get your thoughts down on paper' routine") with "the psychotherapeutic side of writing instruction"; attributes difficulties in invention to "subconscious phobia"; and suggests that composition's efforts to improve the "flow" of writing will allow student writers to "conquer their self-loathing and turn into happy and well-adjusted little graphomaniacs" (94).

While Fish and Menand's negative portrayals of composition studies are admittedly tongue-in-cheek at times—Menand even suggests that Williams's book "will be helpful mainly as a guide to writing college papers for Dr. Dave" (94)—no such mitigating factor is at work in Heather Mac Donald's (1995) *Public Interest* article[1] "Why Johnny Can't Write," which plays off *Newsweek's* 1975 cover story with the same title announcing the nation's so-called literacy crisis. Mac Donald quickly reveals her ostensible purpose: to condemn composition studies for what she suggests are college students' declining literacy skills: "In the field of writing, today's education is not just an irrelevance, it is positively detrimental to a student's development." In her polemic against composition's supposed role in the decline of literacy, Mac Donald—trained in law and now a fellow at the Manhattan Institute—critiques the outcomes of the Dartmouth Conference and the process movement as a whole: "Dartmouth proponents claimed that improvement in students' linguistic skills need not come through direct training in grammar and style but, rather, would flow incidentally as students experiment with personal and expressive forms of talk and writing." Hence, Mac Donald obviously attributes the decline in literacy to process movement practices like free writing and the emphasis on "growth" in student writing.

Despite Mac Donald's apparent interest in student literacy, however, a close reading of her article reveals her real intention: exposing what she calls the disappearance of "objective measure[s] of coherence and correctness" in writing instruction. In other words, when Mac Donald suggests that "elevating process has driven out standards," by "standards" she means a current-traditional view of grammar, style, and correctness. Thus, when Mac Donald, in an attack on multicultural classrooms and difference, writes, "Every writing theory of the past thirty years has come up with reasons why it's not necessary to teach grammar and style" she is suggesting that composition has abandoned correctness because "grammatical errors signify the author is politically engaged." In asserting that the omission of "correctness" in composition curricula is a function of political decisions on the part of the field, she clarifies her real interest in literacy: a desire for a return to grammar-based instruction and a point of view that sees grammar and usage, style, and correctness as essentially the same—and as part of the same prescriptive instructional method.

The excerpts from Mac Donald, Fish, and Menand point to a common problem in composition studies: Topics about writing, rhetoric, and literacy are often brought up in the public sphere, where they are discussed authoritatively by "experts" outside the field of composition. Without an answering word from scholars within the field, however, compositionists are left out in the cold. How is it possible that Fish and Menand—in remarks about composition that generally go against the theoretical underpinnings of an entire field—are able to claim *the* authoritative word on these topics for an important part of the reading public? How can Mac Donald, in words reminiscent of Fish and Menand, resurrect a current-traditional view of style and grammar under the mistaken guise of "literacy" as well as the process movement? "In a process classroom," she writes, "content eclipses form. The college essay and an eighteen-year-old's personality become one and the same." How are these inaccurate characterizations possible when, according to Paula Mathieu, composition has made a "public turn," with an abundance of scholarship, theory, and writing by teachers and students that addresses, in her words, "'real world' texts, events, or exigencies" (Mathieu 2005, 1)? If composition has, as Mathieu claims, made a public turn (see also Weisser 2002, 43), with topics that hold interest for a broad range of individuals, why have writers like Fish, Menand, and Mac Donald—and *not* composition scholars—become the only ones to speak for the field in the public sphere?

COMPOSITION'S DISPLACED PUBLIC INTELLECTUALS

The answer, I suggest, involves one of the chief dilemmas facing composition studies today—the field's lack of public intellectuals, which Fish (1995), in a different forum, defines as "someone who takes as his or her subject matters of public concern, and *has the public's attention*" (118). A crucial question, then, is, where are composition's public intellectuals, and why does the field need them so urgently today? I am not the first person to pose this question about the dearth of public intellectuals in composition. In a *College English* review essay, Frank Farmer (2002) asks how composition can reconstitute the concept of the public intellectual to achieve its own goals: "How can we define—perhaps more accurately redefine—the public intellectual to meet *our* needs and purposes in *our* moment" (202)? Christian Weisser (2002), whose work on public intellectuals makes up part of Farmer's review, calls on compositionists "to rethink what it means to be an intellectual working in the public sphere today" (121) and suggests that one place to look is in "sites outside the classroom in which this discourse is generated and used" (42). Weisser hypothesizes that in composition, the sites of "public writing" and "service-learning," in his estimation, "might very well become the next dominant focal point around which the teaching of college writing is theorized and imagined" (42).

While Weisser's (2002) observations are promising, he bases his thinking in part on one of Fish's highly problematic claims, that is, "academics, by definition, are not candidates for the role of the public intellectual" (Fish 1995, 118)—an assertion that Fish, by virtue of his public work alone, clearly refutes. In a different context, Richard Posner also counters Fish's contention. In his book *Public Intellectuals: A Study of Decline*, Posner (2001) states, "Being an academic public intellectual is a career, albeit a part-time and loosely structured one" (41), and he goes on to suggest that academics are needed most as public intellectuals in areas that require expertise "beyond the capacity of the journalist or other specialist in communication to supply" (45). Within the context of composition studies, public intellectuals can accurately convey the field's theoretical knowledge about writing to the general public. For instance, when the widely circulated editorial by Fish appeared, it prompted one *New York Times* reader to write and advocate resurrecting the anachronistic practice of "teaching sentence diagramming as a prerequisite to proper writing" (Fahy 2005). Compositionists are ideally situated to counter just this type of public representation. As Weisser suggests, "Public writing consists of more than expressing your opinion about a current topic; it entails being able to make your voice heard on an issue that directly confronts or influences you" (Weisser 2002, 94). Applying this idea to public discourse would certainly answer Farmer's call for composition to recreate the public intellectual to fit its disciplinary needs, and, one might add, the needs of the public.

Given the field's lack of public intellectuals, what might account for the apparent disconnect between the discipline and public discourse? Clearly, the history of composition studies itself, including its gendered beginnings, offers a place to begin to answer that question. As Susan Miller (1991) asserts in *Textual Carnivals*, the field's identity is "deeply embedded in traditional views of women's roles," a fact Miller says has led the field to try to "overcome this ancillary status" and to redefine itself "in more crisply masculine, scientific, terms" (122). In tracing the tendency to identify composition with these qualities, Miller suggests that "like women in early communities that depended on their production of live births, composition teachers were at first necessarily placed where they would accrue subordinate associations that were no less binding than those still imposed on women" (127). Miller's connection of composition teachers to a subordinate status resonates with Michael Warner's notion of a "counterpublic." In his work *Publics and Counterpublics* (2002), Warner, borrowing from Habermas's analysis of the public sphere, suggests that "some publics are defined by their tension with a larger public" and argues that "this type of public is—in effect—a counterpublic." He goes on to state that a counterpublic "maintains, at some level, conscious or not, an awareness of its subordinate status." In addition to sexual minorities, Warner cites "the media of women's culture" (56) as one example of such a counterpublic. For his part, Posner indicates that a gendered divide similar to that postulated by Miller and Warner exists in the realm of public intellectuals as a whole, with women constituting just 15.8 percent of the total number Posner studied (2001, 207). Indeed, if we can extrapolate Posner's statistics to what Miller calls the "female coding" of composition (123), it may help explain the lack of public intellectuals in the profession at large and the predominately male pool of non-composition-trained public intellectuals who seem to "speak for" the field.

In addition to disciplinary associations based on gender—and what Warner might deem composition's status as a counterpublic—composition's sometimes contentious relationship with literary studies, the field to which Fish and Menand belong, may account for what often appears to be the absence of recognition for composition's independent disciplinary expertise. Thus, for example, in explaining the field to the public, Menand, a literary scholar who has taught composition, reveals his lack of knowledge of composition's theoretical underpinnings. Worse yet, he depicts the profession as one without any theory to be taken seriously. Fish (2005), meanwhile, in addition to attempting a kind of one-upmanship of composition studies through his "form is the way" approach, implies that composition is not doing its pedagogical job: "Students can't write clean English sentences because they are not being taught what sentences are." While compositionists may be tempted to discount these characterizations from those whose scholarship falls outside the field, Menand's critique nonetheless gains the patina of legitimacy by virtue of his role as a respected Pulitzer Prize-winning author and *New Yorker* writer, while Fish's proposal, as reflected in responses from readers, seems to be enthusiastically embraced. It's evident that a well-educated audience is hearing Fish's and Menand's views with no comparable response from composition professionals. This public discourse shows what happens to disciplinary ethos when compositionists become merely "these new writing clinicians" (Menand 2000, 92) under the acerbic pen of public intellectuals with an attentive audience.

THE ROLE OF STYLE

What has brought about this state of affairs? Why as a profession are we still searching for a valid *public* forum in which to express our views? If we accept Fish's definition of the public intellectual as someone who takes up matters "of public concern," the issue seems clear: As a field, we have not addressed those topics the public cares most deeply about and, as a result, to use Fish's corollary, we do not have the public's ear. What are the topics that most concern a public audience? Even a cursory analysis of Menand's review, Fish's editorial, Mac Donald's *Public Interest* piece, and regular public pronouncements on the decline of reading and writing offers a plausible answer: the areas that seem to be of chief concern outside the field are literacy, style, and grammar and usage. While much of the outcry over reading and writing issues seems to fall under the province of literacy, I argue that style, often viewed through the lens of literacy or grammar and usage, is of paramount importance. Mac Donald's article, for instance, suggests her interest—albeit a narrow, reductive one—in style. Menand (2000) seems to care most about the grammatical aspects of writing when he suggests that using red ink or lowering a grade for confusing "it's" as the possessive of "it" amounts to "using a flyswatter on an ox" (92). Yet, his deft use of metaphor here actually shows his reliance on style. Similarly, Menand approaches the topics of "voice" and imitation (aspects of style) when he critiques "Dr. Dave's" preference for "voices that are out there," like Camille Paglia's: "It is not completely settled that even Camille Paglia should write like Camille Paglia; what can be said with confidence is that she is not a writer whom college students would be prudent to imitate" (94).

The problem of style and the public intellectual is thus paradoxical: the very areas that seem to be of chief concern outside the field are generally disdained or ignored inside it. Our disciplinary abandonment of style in particular, I argue, has precipitated the incursion of the public intellectual into composition studies. Put differently, in its neglect of style as a topic of serious scholarly inquiry (as well as grammar and literacy, to varying degrees), the discipline of composition and rhetoric has ceded the discussion to others outside the field—generally to self-described public intellectuals like Menand, Fish, Mac Donald, and others. Hence, by adopting a hands-off approach to the study of style—and without putting forth our own group of public intellectuals to articulate composition's theories and practices—the field is left with popular, and often erroneous, views that have displaced our own. This situation is part of a scenario that has led composition studies itself to adopt a reductive characterization of style, that is, as merely equivalent to certain current-traditional conceptions of grammar, usage, or punctuation (similar to Mac Donald's, for instance). While compositionists do resist such portrayals—especially in light of our broader rhetorical knowledge of stylistic practices and recent scholarship on style (see, for example, Connors 1997, 2000; Johnson 2003; Micciche 2004; Johnson and Pace 2005;

Duncan 2007)—the field is, at the same time, paralyzed by it, powerless to refute popular, often reductive characterizations for which there is no public counterargument.

In light of this impasse, I propose that it is time for composition and rhetoric to take back the study of style—to redefine the way the conversation is being framed and to rethink that concept in the public sphere. The urgency of this "call to style" goes beyond a desire to reanimate stylistic practices in composition. Indeed, it implicates the politics of the entire field. I contend that one reason composition has been unable to make its case publicly in virtually *any* arena of scholarship or practice, including literacy, is that it has failed to address the study of style (or to articulate a clear position on the difficult-to-limit area of grammar). Regrettably, our neglect comes at our own peril. In failing to articulate ideas about those language topics in which the public seems most invested, the discipline is left without sufficient credibility to bring up other concerns it considers pressing. What's more, this lack of response from composition-trained public intellectuals makes it difficult to dispel pejorative constructions of the field—or downright neglect—from outsiders who treat composition as less than the transformative discipline it is. To reiterate, if one analyzes the nature of the public discourse on language issues, the majority of that discourse arguably concerns the study of style, often appearing in the form of grammar, punctuation, and literacy. When style is discussed, it is frequently associated with current-traditional approaches to the topic (e.g., see Mac Donald 1995). To counter this tendency, it is essential for the field to go public with a renewed emphasis on style and to employ its disciplinary expertise.

While composition as a discipline has recently expressed some renewed interest in the study of style, it seems safe to say that, since around 1985, the field as a whole has largely ignored stylistic theory and practice and rendered it invisible. In fact, even as the study of style multiplied during the Golden Age, some were already retrospectively labeling it a "static" practice or including it as part of "current-traditional rhetoric." Mac Donald's

Public Interest article attempts to make just that association while advocating the superiority of a product-based approach. Yet, I contend that the association of style with current-traditional rhetoric is not historically accurate (see Chap. 3). This period of style's ascendancy also included the development of what Connors (2000) has called "sentence-based rhetorics" (98) or the practices of sentence combining, generative rhetoric, and rhetorical imitation, the first two largely concerned with syntax. Connors questions the disappearance of these stylistic practices from composition theory and pedagogy and begins the tangible reemergence of discussions about the role of style in the field. T. R. Johnson's (2003) *A Rhetoric of Pleasure: Prose Style and Today's Composition Classroom* and Johnson and Tom Pace's (2005) *Refiguring Prose Style: Possibilities for Writing Pedagogy* offer an eclectic approach to studying style, while Richard Lanham's (2006) *The Economics of Attention: Style and Substance in the Age of Information* makes the claim that style and substance have, in effect, been reversed as we vie for attention in a technologically oriented society. Lanham writes, "If attention is now at the center of the economy rather than fluff, then so is style. It moves from the periphery to the center" (xi–xii).

THE STATUS OF GRAMMAR IN COMPOSITION STUDIES

In 2006, the WPA listserv responded quickly when an article about grammar instruction appeared in the *Washington Post.* In "Clauses and Commas Make a Comeback: SAT Helps Return Grammar to Class," staff writer Daniel de Vise (2006) features a high-school English teacher in Virginia who has resurrected "direct grammar instruction"—in other words, noncontextual grammar drills—in his classes, apparently in response to the new writing section of the SAT that consists primarily of grammar questions. Perhaps the most controversial aspect of the article is an erroneous assertion de Vise makes about a supposed change in NCTE's policy on grammar: "The National Council of Teachers of English, whose directives shape curriculum decisions nationwide, has quietly reversed its long opposition to grammar drills, which the group had condemned in 1985 as 'a deterrent to the improvement of students' speaking and writing.'" As NCTE President Kathleen Blake Yancey (2006) wrote on WPA after the *Post* article appeared, "This claim—that NCTE has changed its stance on grammar—is false, and we've spent the better part of the day trying to get it corrected. . . . You spend hours and hours trying to get some attention paid to what you stand for, and this is what they pick up. And of course, it would be about grammar." While de Vise (2006) fails to cite specific authority for this claim, the article does quote Amy Benjamin of the Assembly for the Teaching of English Grammar, a group affiliated with NCTE, who tells de Vise that "our time has come." However, Benjamin's group—which de Vise says has evolved into "standard bearers" on language issues—does not speak for the national organization of NCTE, and is clearly at odds with NCTE on this issue.

It is important to acknowledge the extent to which the so-called "grammar question" remains particularly vexed in a field that has approached the subject with ambivalence for some time. For years, the study of style has overlapped with the discourse of grammar in a number of crucial respects. What de Vise's *Post* article shows, however, is that the public discourse about grammar tends to revive and, indeed, promote a prescriptive approach that the field officially abandoned long ago. Yet, even Menand (2000) assumes grammar's centrality to the field when he tries to dispel some "grammatical superstitions" and then goes on to discuss the composition teacher's "almost hopeless task of undoing this tangle of hearsay and delusion [that grammar and usage involve]" (92). Ironically, Menand's review is concerned primarily with stylistic issues—not the grammatical ones with which they are often confused or conflated. Indeed, the continued misunderstanding of composition's position on grammar suggests that this is another area in which the field could profit by clearly articulating a public position. Any effort to do so, however, would require an examination of the history of composition's relationship with grammar, including the importance of Patrick Hartwell's (1985) article "Grammar,

Grammars, and the Teaching of Grammar" in which the author suggests that there are five different definitions of grammar, succinctly summarized by David Blakesley (1995) as follows:

> (1) the set of formal patterns in which the words of a language are arranged in order to convey larger meanings; (2) linguistic grammar, which studies these formal patterns; (3) linguistic etiquette (usage . . . which is not grammar, per se); (4) school grammar (the grammar of textbooks); and (5) stylistic grammar (grammatical terms used to teach style). (195)

In his conclusion, which echoes some of the findings of a 1963 NCTE study by Richard Braddock, Richard Lloyd-Jones, and Lowell Schoer, Hartwell (1985) argues that teaching formal grammar out of context does not help and in fact can harm the teaching of writing. He states, "One learns to control the language of print by manipulating language in meaningful contexts, not by learning about language in isolation, as by the study of formal grammar" (125). That claim, it seems, has remained the field's leitmotif on the role of grammar in composition instruction, as NCTE's position statement affirms. Even though Hartwell's conclusion that both style and grammar are inherently rhetorical may be accepted by most compositionists, however, I contend that when the "grammar question" arises in the public arena, it is not enough simply to reiterate Hartwell's conclusions. Instead, I argue that the field must publicly articulate a view of grammar that others can better relate to and understand. Is it possible, as compositionist Janet Zepernick seems to imply on the WPA listserv, that our often visceral reactions to public assertions about grammar have contributed to our invisibility within the public sphere?

> One of the public relations problems we face as a discipline is that instead of responding to the pro-grammar movement among non-comps by saying, "Yes, we see what you want. We call it X, and here's how we do it and why it works so well when we do it this way," we've generally responded by circling the wagons and writing diatribes against the grammar police. (Zepernick 2005)

Zepernick's concerns seem precisely on point, especially in light of the regular recurrence of the topic in what might be called composition studies' "private" sphere, the WPA listserv. In addition to discussions of the recent article on teaching grammar in high schools, list members responded en masse in 2004 when David Mulroy (2003), in *The War against Grammar*, directly took on NCTE and what Mulroy considered the professional organization's position that "instruction in formal grammar did not accomplish any positive goals" (15). Mulroy is effectively attacking NCTE's official adoption of the Braddock, Lloyd-Jones, and Schoer (1963) position that "the teaching of formal grammar has a negligible, or, because it usually displaces some instruction and practice in composition, even a harmful effect on improvement in writing" (37–38). NCTE's position so incensed Mulroy that, according to a review of the book, the author "set aside his special interest, translating Latin and Greek poetry, and devoted several years to researching the history of the study of grammar" (Reedy 2003, 15). In his book, Mulroy argues that university professors have ignored grammar instruction for the past 75 years and that the United States should adopt a policy similar to England's National Literacy Strategy, which offers workshops for teachers "deficient" in their knowledge of grammar and punctuation. Nick Carbone's (2004) response to the discussion on WPA-L is representative of compositionists' position:

> There is no war against grammar. There is instead a struggle to teach writing. That's a different thing. In that struggle we've come to believe, based on sound evidence and experience, that grammar in isolation, rules-only, skill and drill as the best approach for learning the basics of writing doesn't work. So teaching grammar for grammar's sake in a course that's a writing course or meant to help students write better, we're not for. (WPA-L, February 25, 2004)

In the aftermath of the WPA listserv discussion of *The War on Grammar*, Joe Hardin summarized his view of the field's complicated position on questions of grammar and style. Hardin

(2004) goes beyond Carbone's statement to express the centripetal effect of the term "grammar" as it draws a host of disparate ideas within its nomenclature, making it difficult for the field to articulate its position clearly:

> It's really a complex argument that is linked to the whole contemporary language theory. Many believe that it's an argument against standards. It's not. Many believe that it suggests that we abandon style and syntax and sentence-level work completely. It doesn't. It's mostly an argument against the traditional way of teaching "grammar" and the goals of that tradition. It's an argument for a correction of terms and what those terms imply—what traditional books teach is "usage," not grammar, for instance. It's an argument against the transferability of the rules-example-exercises approach to the production of good writing. (WPA-L, March 10, 2004)

As Hardin suggests, the study of style (including syntax and sentence-level work) often gets indiscriminately wrapped up in the field's general prohibition against formal noncontextualized grammar instruction. In other words, we have come to confuse style and grammar, conflating it in the same way that those without disciplinary training do. What's more, because the field has adopted various rhetorical approaches to grammar that fall more accurately under the rubric of style, my discussion of the field's response to grammar—to the extent I discuss it here—relates to the study of style. In his article, Hartwell himself treats style (what he calls "stylistic grammar" or "Grammar 5") differently from his other four categories of grammar and makes it clear that style is useful in ways that grammar *per se* is not. In fact, in his discussion of stylistic grammar, Hartwell (1985) writes, "When we turn to Grammar 5 . . . we find that the grammar issue is simply beside the point" (124).

STYLE, GRAMMAR, LITERACY, AND STUDENTS' RIGHT TO THEIR OWN LANGUAGE

Part of the fate of style, grammar, and literacy in the field today originates in an important document promulgated by the

Committee on CCCC Language in 1974, the "Students' Right to Their Own Language." The resolution on language begins: "We affirm the students' right to their own patterns and varieties of language—the dialects of their nurture or whatever dialects in which they find their own identity and style" (Committee on CCCC Language 1974, 2). CCCC's adoption of the Students' Right resolution, with its affirmation of the diversity of literacy, style, and grammar in a multicultural society, precedes by a year *Newsweek's* "Why Johnny Can't Write" issue (1975), which has resonated in the public sphere for decades (see, for instance, Mac Donald's 1995 article with the same title). In short, the connection between writing and "non-standard" dialects that the "Students' Right to Their Own Language" supports has dictated disciplinary policy and thinking ever since. Among the points made in the document is that content should be emphasized: "If we can convince our students that spelling, punctuation, and usage are less important than content, we have removed a major obstacle in their developing the ability to write" (Committee on CCCC Language 1974, 8). The statement about the importance of content is clearly at odds with Fish's (2005) statement about form's paramount place in composition classes and may explain compositionists' response to Fish's op-ed piece. What's more, the Students' Right document, with its emphasis on content, may also help explain the resistance to style within the field itself. Paradoxically, however, what perhaps no one has recognized up to this point is that the Students' Right document is fundamentally—and has been since its inception—an explicit and implicit call to style for the field.

In other words, the "Students' Right" resolution proposes an interpretation of dialect, variation, and other language matters that suggests, in short, not only an explicit view of style—that is, "students' right to their own patterns and varieties of language . . . in which they find their own identity and style"—but an innovative one as well. The authors write that "in every composition class there are examples of writing which is clear and vigorous despite the use of non-standard forms . . . and there are certainly many examples of limp, vapid writing in 'standard dialect'" (8). It seems evident, then, that if composition as a field embraces the idea of difference in various dialects, that idea is inextricably linked to the idea of variation as a fundamental aspect of style. Thus, it is crucial that compositionists rethink the idea of style in conjunction with "Students' Right to Their Own Language"—rather than in opposition to it. Along the same lines, the authors of the Students' Right document are effectively making an argument for style (while not necessarily calling it that) when they discuss the importance of embracing difference in student writing. That admonition occurs when the document describes writing in nonuniform dialects:

> Many of us have taught as though the function of schools and colleges were to erase differences. Should we, on the one hand, urge creativity and individuality in the arts and the sciences, take pride in the diversity of our historical development, and, on the other hand, try to obliterate all the differences in the way Americans speak and write? Our major emphasis has been on uniformity, in both speech and writing; would we accomplish more, both educationally and ethically, if we shifted that emphasis to precise, effective, and appropriate communication in diverse ways, whatever the dialect? (2)

Indeed, as the Students' Right document suggests, the question of whether the form of a person's dialect or home language can be separated from its content—and content in this case implicates a person's very identity—continues to trouble composition as a discipline. Thus, "Students' Right to Their Own Language" reflects the continuing relevance of the most important issue in style theory.

As part of reanimating style in composition, then, the field ought to draw more on the "Students' Right to Their Own Language" and the guidance it offers. Now almost thirty-five years old, the document often seems to go unnoticed. In terms of its reception in the public sphere, it arguably serves as the basis of misconceptions about how the field treats writing and how it has construed the very nature of difference with respect to language, dialect, and style. Within composition studies itself, the document, unwittingly perhaps, has given impetus to a reductive view of style that is, ironically, just the opposite of what the document's authors envision. It has perhaps produced an internal tension within the field that would, if explored more fully, help composition and rhetoric articulate far more clearly a position that could reinvigorate interpretations of style—and of the field—in the public sphere.

COMPLICATING "CLARITY" IN THE PUBLIC SPHERE

As "Students' Right to Their Own Language" suggests, the field of composition has a number of innovative ideas with respect to language that should be introduced in the public sphere, if only because they challenge conventional wisdom. One example of this is the complication of the notion of "clarity," which is often taken as a given not only in public discourse, but in the field, as well. Consider, for instance, Mac Donald's (1995) *Public Interest* article, which begins with the assertion that "the only thing composition teachers are not talking and writing about these days is how to teach students to compose clear, logical prose." Mac Donald's emphasis on clarity in writing is echoed by Menand (2000), who gives a list of speech characteristics that writing teachers should help students eliminate from their writing "in the interest of clarity"; these include "repetition, contradiction, exaggeration, run-ons, fragments, and clichés, plus an array of tonal and physical inflections—drawls, grunts, shrugs, winks, hand gestures—unreproducible in written form" (94). Yet, the idea of clarity is, in fact, more problematic than Menand or Mac Donald allows. At least one composition scholar, Richard Lanham, began to question the common assumptions about clarity as early as 1974. Recognizing that the term "clarity" itself is impossible to define (because it is a rhetorical concept that shifts), Lanham (1974) writes, "Obviously, there can be no single verbal pattern that can be called 'clear.' All depends on context—social, historical, attitudinal" (33). Lanham reveals the chief principle he sees at work in most theories of clarity:

the tendency to want to make writing transparent, or to have it seem invisible to those reading it, as if it points to some definitive underlying reality.

Thus, at least part of the problem in the disappearance of stylistic study, I argue, is that composition has essentially been interpellated by myths regarding clarity as well as other public myths about style. By "interpellation" I mean that there has been a tendency to accept prescriptive standards of grammar, punctuation, and style that support a reductive view of the canon. By "myths" I mean that frequent repetition makes the so-called "rules" take on a life of their own, raising them to the level of prescription. As an example, in opposition to what many claim as the inherent transparency of a clear style, Lanham proposes instead the idea of an opaque style that calls attention to itself. He states, "Either we notice an opaque style as a *style* (i.e., we look *at* it) or we do not (i.e., we look *through* it to a fictive reality beyond)" (Lanham 1983b, 58). Lanham recognizes that an opaque style is seen as "the enemy of clarity" and that a binary has developed favoring a clear or transparent style. "Transparent styles, because they go unnoticed, are good," he writes. "Opaque styles, which invite stylistic self-consciousness, are bad" (47, 59).

Lanham's theory thus complicates the notion of clarity in writing in important ways. He argues persuasively that the injunction to "be clear" refers "not to words on a page but to responses, yours or your reader's" (Lanham 1983a, 2). In another nod at the inherently rhetorical nature of the concept, he goes on to suggest that the idea of clarity indicates how successful a writer might be in getting his or her audience "to share our view of the world, a view we have composed by perceiving it" (3). In *Publics and Counterpublics,* Warner offers a similarly rhetorical view of clarity: "It could be argued that the imperative to write clearly is not the same as the need to write accessibly, that even difficult styles can have the clarity of precision" (139).[2] Warner and Lanham's highly contextual views of clarity, however, differ markedly from the normal "take" on the notion, especially in the public sphere, where many writers, like Menand and Mac Donald, accept as a given its relative merits. Lanham's view, on the other hand, reveals that the concept of clarity is not as simple as it generally seems, but is extremely complex and difficult to explain in a style manual or an easy-to-digest formula. If we take Lanham's argument seriously, then, the major proscriptions against "muddy" writing become mere shibboleths that displace more nuanced positions in composition studies about what it means to "be clear."

The reason it is important to articulate such a position is that the meaning of "good writing" in the field is ultimately at stake. As Warner points out, the common conception is that "writing that is unclear to nonspecialists is just 'bad writing'" (138). Yet if style is not opaque or "ornamental"—in other words, if it does not call attention to itself in any way—then all that is left for us to discuss regarding "good" writing are the prescriptive views of clarity (and other myths) regularly reproduced both outside and inside the field. Taken to its logical conclusion, then, this conception of clarity implies that a clear style *has* no style and serves only as a mirror to an underlying meaning. This unquestioned acceptance of a transparent style, as Lanham points out, has read out of the equation any potentially interesting notions of an opaque or self-conscious style. As the clarity discussion demonstrates, the perpetuation of popular myths about style has unwittingly held the field hostage, rendering it unable to move beyond certain public perceptions despite the efforts of scholars like Lanham to challenge their underlying rationale and use. Indeed, in the public sphere, the field of composition might point to writing styles that are complex, nuanced, and yet highly effective at complicating and enriching the discussion of difficult ideas. Composition scholars could use the public sphere as a forum in which to explain the value of styles that may not, at first glance, appear transparent or clear to most people.

One instance where the explanation of a complex, yet meaningful style would have been helpful is in a "Readings" section of *Harper's Magazine* (Vitanza 1994) that quickly betrays its real purpose: to make its subject, composition professor Victor Vitanza—and, in turn, the field itself—seem vain, inarticulate, and, in the form in which it's presented, unclear. In "Reading, Writing, Rambling On," the *Harper's* (1994) piece undermines Vitanza by taking excerpts from his larger interview in *Composition Studies* (1993) conducted by Cynthia Haynes-Burton, without giving the broader context for his ideas. When, for instance, Haynes-Burton asks, "Who do you think your audience is?" Vitanza's theoretical response, reprinted in *Harper's*, shows some of his conflicted sense of the field: "I am always giving writing lessons and taking writing lessons. I don't know, however, if I am Levi-Strauss or if I am that South-American Indian chief in *Tristes Tropiques* that Levi-Strauss indirectly gives writing lessons to. Perhaps I am both. Which can be confusing" (29). On the surface, of course, Vitanza's (1994) statements appear opaque, even comical, even though they are arguably a stylistic tour de force in which the author uses the rhetorical trope of *periphrasis* to show the difficulty of capturing the rhetorical situation of literacy, which he names "inappropriation" (1993, 52). Yet, the *Harper's* excerpt does not capture Vitanza's dilemma or his uncertain relationship with the very notion of "audience," which he examines at length in the *Composition Studies* piece. In a portion of that interview omitted in *Harper's*, Vitanza states, "I think that audiences are really overrated!" (1993, 51), and one solution, he explains, is to rethink the relationship between writers and audiences.

Later, after Vitanza expresses doubts about how he positions himself as a researcher in the field, Haynes-Burton asks him to "please start over," and Vitanza's conflicted reply includes the following paragraph reproduced in *Harper's* (1994):

> Okay, so what I have said so far: I very consciously do not follow the field's research protocols. And yet, of course, I do; most other times, however, I do not. And yet again! Do you feel the vertigo of this? I hope that my saying all this, however, does not come across as if I

> am disengaging into some form of "individualism," or "expressionism," for I do not believe in such a fatuous, dangerous concept as practiced in our field (29).

In the context of the full interview in *Composition Studies*, Vitanza expresses the point of view that as a field, composition has always been positioned among research protocols borrowed from various disciplinary interests, and he is acknowledging how, as a scholar allied with postmodern theory, he is torn trying both to conform to and resist those protocols. Yet, by focusing on these contradictory positions without giving additional context, the magazine attempts to ridicule Vitanza's equivocation. Nonetheless, his words express brilliantly the lack of clarity he obviously feels on this subject. Likewise, the debate over expressionism in the field is complicated by years of disciplinary discussion, and while Vitanza is in a camp that might indeed label expressionism "fatuous," the *Harper's* excerpt provides none of the background necessary for readers to understand its historical complexity, making the scholar again seem out of touch with the field—and certainly with his audience.

ONGOING DISCIPLINARY DIVISION

While much of the misunderstanding about the role of style in composition comes from outside the field, the abandonment of the study of style has led to the perpetuation of certain preconceptions from within the discipline as well. In a *College English* opinion piece, for example, Peter Elbow (2002), one of composition's best-known scholars, suggests that style is now almost exclusively a part of the "culture" of literary studies. In "The Cultures of Literature and Composition: What Could Each Learn from the Other?" Elbow, calling for a kind of revival of style in composition, suggests that currently it is literature—and *not* composition—that has "a culture that considers the metaphorical and imaginative uses of language as basic or primal" (536). In other words, Elbow suggests, the discipline of literary studies has become in essence *the* province of style:

> The culture of literary studies puts a high value on style and on not being like everyone else. I think I see more mannerism, artifice, and self-consciousness in bearing . . . among literary folk than composition folk. Occasionally I resist, yet I value style and artifice. What could be more wonderful than the pleasure of creating or appreciating forms that are different, amazing, outlandish, useless—the opposite of ordinary, everyday, pragmatic? (542)

Granted, Elbow does not go so far as to dismiss the role composition plays in a so-called culture of style. However, his acknowledgment that the "culture of composition" does not ignore "metaphor and imaginative language *altogether*" is really so much damnation with faint praise (536; emphasis added). Echoing in important respects the same assumptions often made about the field in the public sphere, he says that composition generally adopts a "literal language . . . that seems to assume discursive language as the norm and imaginative, metaphorical language as somehow special or marked or additional" (536). Elbow's concept of style is, of course, somewhat circumscribed in this instance, even though he suggests, as Lanham does, that style has an opaque quality he considers desirable. It's clear that Elbow is advocating a revival of style, yet instead of looking at style's important roots in composition, the only model he considers is literature.

By locating stylistic studies almost exclusively within the domain of literature, however, and by dichotomizing "literary" and "discursive" language, Elbow effectively initiates a "divide" or schism between literature and composition that mimics the divide between popular and academic views of style in the public arena. In other words, Elbow seems to create a public within a public (see Warner's "counterpublic") in the academic realm itself. Like Fish, Menand, and Mac Donald, however—and indeed, as I have argued, like composition studies as a whole—Elbow is failing to account for the broad body of scholarship on style in the field. For example, as Lanham, Edward P. J. Corbett, and others have pointed out, a wide variety of rhetorical figures (e.g., tropes and schemes) has been used throughout the history of stylistic studies and in the teaching of writing. Furthermore, by dividing literary or poetic style from what he labels composition's supposed focus—which he regrettably calls an "orientation toward grammar"—Elbow clearly adopts a view challenged not only by many scholars in the field itself (see, for example, Hartwell 1985; Carbone 2004; Hardin 2004), but by linguist Mary Louise Pratt. In *Toward a Speech Act Theory of Literary Discourse*, Pratt (1977) critiques that very binary when she argues that the supposed division between "poetic" and "non-poetic" language is based on an unverifiable split between poetic language (the language of literature) and linguistics (everyday language, the so-called "discursive" language Elbow refers to as the province of composition).

According to Pratt, this "poetic language fallacy" is a false division because it presupposes certain elements unique to literary or poetic language and ostensibly nonexistent in nonpoetic language. Pratt essentially challenges the claims of the Prague Circle—a group of linguists and writers interested in language in Russia during the 1930s—that there is a metaphorical *langue/parole* relationship unique to literature: "The fact that . . . there is a real *langue* shared by literary and nonliterary utterances alike is quite overlooked and seems almost irrelevant" (10). She goes on to argue that the faulty analogy between *langue* (as literary) and *parole* (as nonliterary) has widespread implications for style and underlies "the overwhelming tendency to view style as an exclusively or predominantly literary phenomenon and *to equate style outside literature with mere grammaticality and conventional appropriateness*" (15; emphasis added). Clearly, this is the very separation that Elbow makes when he writes about the difference between literary and conventional discourse (i.e., the discourse of composition).

Even though I obviously share Elbow's claim that there is a problematic absence of attention to style in composition, I do not see the stylistic schism he hypothesizes between composition and literary studies. Instead, I argue, the problem is the inability of compositionists to articulate a clear view of the value of stylistic study in the field. Elbow suggests that the existence of a gap in stylistic study is currently filled by literary studies. Yet, it is evident that public intellectuals outside the field—many of whom are not literary scholars—are filling this gap in their own way. Elbow, like Menand and others, simply represents a different instantiation of the same disciplinary problem: the inability of composition to use and articulate its longstanding knowledge base. The field clearly has a rich tradition in the study of style. By reclaiming it, composition studies has nothing to lose and much to gain, both immediately and over the long term, in asserting knowledge about practices of style that have a rich disciplinary history. Illuminating those stylistic traditions for the public would give the field a claim to the very expertise held by composition scholars. It would establish the importance of composition studies by reclaiming language concerns that are important both inside and outside the field. Compositionists would be seen as public intellectuals with valuable theoretical positions on an array of language matters, including stylistic ones.

RESPONDING IN THE PUBLIC SPHERE

If the field of composition is to write in the public sphere, it has to start somewhere. I begin that process here by responding to Fish, Menand, Mac Donald, and others who have represented the field—often inaccurately, in my view—in the public sphere. I aim to show the benefit of writing as a public intellectual in public discourse.

In making the argument that form in composition courses is more important than content, Fish is stating a notion that is far from new—yet incorrect. Why? For years, a form/content dichotomy has existed, with form considered by some—like Fish—as a container that can be filled with any content. The idea that form (which includes style, structure, grammar, and so forth) can thus be separated from content led composition scholar Louis Milic to propose a dualistic view in the 1960s that he called the "theory of ornate form." Milic (1965) states that form is separate from, and, he implies, more important than, content because "ideas exist wordlessly and can be dressed in a variety of outfits depending on the need or the occasion" (67). For Milic, then (and we can assume Fish agrees), the opposite idea, which states that form and content are inseparable because the two are an "organic" whole, is erroneous. If this organic theory, which he calls "Crocean aesthetic monism," were correct, writes Milic, and there were, in fact, "no seam between meaning and style," then even a small change in form would necessarily mean a change in content—and that implies there *is* no form (or style) but only "meaning or intuition" (67). Milic claims that ornate form is the only theory that allows composition instructors to teach style by making it separate from content.

However, Milic's idea is mistaken: form (style) and content (meaning) are actually inextricably linked, and here is the reason why. While it's true that ideas can be put in any number of ways—indeed, this is the very notion of style—what Milic and Fish both overlook is that the form itself carries meaning. How so? When Fish dismisses content, he is assuming that words carry only a denotative (or explicit) meaning. This denotative meaning, like the form/content division itself, is based on a positivist assumption that sees language narrowly in terms of one possible transparent meaning. However, much of what we take to be meaning is not denotative at all. Rather, it is connotative (suggested or implied) and comes from various rhetorical elements—e.g., humor, irony or sarcasm, emphasis, and even ethos, or the credibility/character of the writer—as well as cultural and social understandings, and thus a great deal of connotative meaning is conveyed through *form.* Form itself, then, often expresses meaning above and beyond the denotative meaning. Take Fish, for example. His column for the *Chronicle of Higher Education,* written before his *Times* piece, is entitled "Say It Ain't So" (2002), an ironic title that in its lexical choice ("Ain't"), its register (colloquial), and its use of allusion (a kind of cultural "gotcha") conveys, through form, a great deal about his resistance to conventional wisdom. This is an instance, then, when form, which is clearly significant in and of itself, works in conjunction with meaning, including the prior meanings attached to this expression without which the title itself would have a different meaning. Indeed, if Fish were to teach his students the way form can be used to alter meaning, it seems that he might reach a different conclusion from his decision to banish content from his classroom teaching.

If one idea could be said to characterize Menand's ideas in his *New Yorker* review, it would likely be his reliance on psychoanalytical theory to describe the process of writing in composition classrooms. As a matter of fact, issues of writing have long been tied to psychology, especially in the study of the writing process. Yet, comparing writing to issues of psychotherapy is rare. It is true that in a special double issue of *College English* on psychoanalysis and pedagogy, guest editor Robert Con Davis (1987) concludes that "the problematics of psychoanalytic therapy (defined by 'resistance,' 'transference,' and 'repression') are the same as 'the problematics of teaching'" (622), and Menand's ideas seem informed by similar considerations. Yet, when he talks about writing pedagogy as a "combination of psychotherapy and social work" (92), Menand (2000) is actually more interested in portraying composition in one light—as influenced by the theory of expressivism, or a movement that focuses on the idea that writing involves exploring personal experience and voice. The expressivist movement has generated a great deal of debate even in composition, as Vitanza's repudiation of it indicates, but Menand, as well as Mac Donald, confuse readers with their insistence that expressivist rhetoric, not to mention process, are the enemies of grammar and style.

This is where an important explanation is useful: Menand's and Mac Donald's characterizations of the field assume a view of writing based on current-traditional rhetoric, which emphasizes product over process, as Fish (2005) does in his *New York Times* op-ed piece. Current-traditional rhetoric is concerned with, among other things, grammar, usage, and mechanics—essentially aspects of language affiliated with the textual product rather than with the process of producing it. Menand's critique of the so-called psychotherapeutic approaches (voice, freewriting, drafting, revision, etc.)—along with Mac Donald's criticism of the Dartmouth Conference—basically amount to the same thing: a desire to return to a strict emphasis on the textual product and to throw out the process writers use to achieve it. Why is that harmful? Research has shown that all of the techniques associated with "process" are useful to writers in accomplishing their writing goals. They are productive not only for student writers, but for professional writers as well. The process movement has never ignored the textual product, but has looked at the individual, social, cultural, and public considerations that make up the text. When they write about the field, however, Menand and Mac Donald do not take these considerations into account, and therefore they dismiss a great deal of useful knowledge that has been acquired by writers and teachers over time.

It is the job of composition studies to develop writing through many processes. In doing so, the field shares the same goals as Fish, Menand, Mac Donald, and others who have portrayed us in public: to produce excellence in writing. Like these public intellectuals, we want to help writers compose with attention to style and contextually appropriate grammar and vocabulary. However, we have discovered methods for achieving good writing that allow writers to take into account the way they arrive at their product. Along the way, both form and content—and everything that goes along with these concepts—are important to composition professionals and should be to all writers and readers everywhere.

6

BACK IN STYLE

Style and the Future of Composition Studies

Several years ago, I spent more than 100 hours in one of the tiny basement rooms that make up the language laboratory at Middlebury College in Vermont. Using a machine that allowed me to hear my own voice simultaneously juxtaposed with the native French speakers on the tapes, I practiced some of the sounds most difficult for Americans to master: the vocalic /r/, the nasal /u/ sound that does not exist in English, and its contrast with the /ou/ sound that is slightly more rounded and not quite like any comparable sound in English. I also practiced the rhythm of the language, since French intonation is flat, without the rise and fall of accented syllables that exist in every word in English. What I did not realize at the time is that my language lab experience was a study of style, the rehearsal of phonological aspects of the French language that contribute to meaning. In my language practice, I also focused—for the most part tacitly—on other stylistic features: syntax, or the word order in sentences; lexical features, especially variations in vocabulary and the agreement of nouns, including pronouns, with masculine or feminine genders; and register, the different levels of formality that often were signaled by the use of a formal pronoun for "you" (*vous*) in contrast with the informal pronoun (*tu*).

While some exceptions exist, the language lab in many American colleges and universities today has largely become an artifact, part of language teaching and learning replaced by other technological, pedagogical, and theoretical practices. I argue that the study of style has suffered the same fate, its value increasingly lost as style theory and practice have come to represent a kind of anachronism in the field of composition. That fate, I maintain, is both undeserved and unfortunate.

Like the wide range of voices I listened to and learned from in the language laboratory, the study of style offers new language resources for writers. The explicit knowledge of those resources—rhetorical, linguistic, and extending into discourse—can help writers to create and express meaning as language effects. I acknowledge that this is not always a conscious process and that some writers may deploy style effectively without explicit knowledge of its resources. In fact, given the dearth of style studies today, I suspect that many writers use stylistic features without any overt knowledge of them. Nevertheless, just as an athlete with a natural sense of how to play a sport may improve his or her ability after seeing his or her performance on videotape, so a writer, armed with an arsenal of stylistic features, may look at his or her writing with new understandings and develop, adapt, or appropriate new composing strategies.

If we accept the premise that the neglect of stylistic resources by the field has precluded conscious knowledge of valuable language practices, I argue that this loss is the result of composition's fundamental misunderstanding of the role of style in its past studies, pedagogies, disciplinary practices, and history. I have suggested that misunderstanding comes from the field's *retrospective* tendency (1) to affiliate an emphasis on style with current-traditional rhetoric and (2) to see style as the antithesis of invention, even though evidence shows that neither characterization is accurate. In associating style with current-traditional rhetoric—a term that has acquired negative connotations over the years—and thereby discounting it, we have failed to see the study of style for what it actually represented during composition's process movement: a set of innovative practices used to generate and express language through the deployment of rhetorical features. In losing the natural connection shared by the canons of style and invention at that time, we no longer look for ways in which they could be used profitably together in current discourse. While the two canons are often seen as independent, their dichotomization disallows the possibility of an inventional style, the kind scholars demonstrated through the development of stylistic practices during the process era and Golden Age.

STYLE AS EMOTIONAL FORM AND MEANING

In addition to looking prospectively at new approaches to the study of style in composition, it is instructive to return to one historically recurrent theoretical problem: whether language can be separated from substance, form from content, style from meaning. What most critics claim is at stake is the answer to the apparently intractable question of whether meaning remains the same if something is said in different ways, through different words. If a writer changes even one word in a sentence, has she in effect changed the entire meaning? In other words, are form and content separate—or inseparable? While various scholars have proposed ways to get around the question, I think the best solution might be to frame the problem somewhat differently. First, it seems clear that the distinction falls apart at the point when the study of style leads to meaning. For example, even if we read something that we remark as having a certain style, later we generally do not remember what we have read verbatim (unless, of course, we have memorized it). Instead, we recall the meaning. At some point, then, and on some level, it seems we must agree that style and meaning necessarily converge. To suggest otherwise is to deny the way in which form and content are inextricably linked in recollection. However, even if this connection is certain, one question that no one has adequately explored is the impact of style on the *kind* of meaning retained. Another question is the effect of style on memory.

In examining the kind of meaning we retain, scholars in the 1970s like Richard Ohmann and Virginia Tufte developed the idea of style as "emotional form." While they looked at the study of style—Tufte specifically explored the way syntax operates—as a way of fulfilling expectations (see Burke 1968), no one has reexamined that question recently. In many ways, however, the notion of style as emotional form that Tufte and Ohmann reinvigorated is fundamentally a question from classical rhetoric, one the Sophists took up in ways later reprised by Cicero and Quintilian (see Chap. 2). To examine that question here, I quote below, in translation, from *My Mother's Castle*, the second volume of a memoir, subtitled *Memories of Childhood*, by French writer and filmmaker Marcel Pagnol (1960). What his nonfiction style evokes for me is an emotional response to a place I have not seen (the environs of Marseilles, France) and a time I did not live through (the early 1900s). How does the author achieve a version of Tufte and Ohmann's "emotional form"? I argue that it is Pagnol's style—his choice of words, syntax, variation of the length and tenor of sentences, use of periodic sentences, and particularly conciseness and amplification in discourse—that controls the nature of the meaning for readers. Thus, if it is true that what remains after the author's actual words are forgotten is the meaning—and the way we remember it—I suggest that meanings are necessarily determined by a writer's emotional style. The excerpt below appears at the end of Pagnol's memoir and recounts, within the space of a few paragraphs, what has happened over the course of approximately 15 years in the author's life:

> Time passes and turns the wheel of life, as water turns the mill-wheel.
>
> •
>
> Five years later, I was walking behind a black carriage, whose wheels were so high that I could see the horses' hooves. I was dressed in black, and young Paul's hand was gripping mine with all its strength. My mother was being borne away for ever.
>
> •
>
> I have no other memory of that dreadful day, as if the fifteen-year old that I was refused to admit a grief so overwhelming that it could have killed me. For years, in fact until we reached manhood, we never had the courage to speak of her.
>
> •
>
> Paul . . . was the last of Virgil's goat-herds. . . . But at the age of thirty he died in a clinic. On his bedside table lay his mouth-organ.

•

> My dear Lili did not walk at my side as I accompanied [Paul] to his little graveyard at La Treille, for he had been waiting for him there for years, under a carpet of immortelles humming with bees; during the war of 1914, in a black northern forest, a bullet in the forehead cut short his young life, and he had sunk, under the falling rain, on a tangle of chilly plants whose names he did not even know.
>
> •
>
> Such is the life of man. A few joys, quickly obliterated by unforgettable sorrows.
>
> •
>
> There is no need to tell the children so. (1960, 338–39)

In this excerpt from Pagnol's memoir, it is important to acknowledge that the words would be meaningless without the current and prior meanings attached to them. In that regard, the reader already has extensive knowledge of Pagnol's mother, brother, and childhood friend, Lili, whose deaths the author recounts here toward the end of the second in a series of two memoirs about Pagnol's childhood (the first is *My Father's Glory* 1960). I propose, however, that when a reader wants to recall the emotion evoked—the "feeling" he or she has about a time, a place, a memory, a history—that feeling is not reproduced simply through its propositional meaning (the meaning that can be evaluated as either true or false, partly from prior knowledge) but through its style. In other words, it is not only the events Pagnol relates about the death of his mother, brother, and Lili that have an impact on the reader, but the emotion conveyed through the stylistic resources Pagnol employs. Style, then, is important because it conveys emotion, enriching meaning beyond denotation to include connotation and nuance. A slightly different approach to the same problem, using terms from speech act theory, suggests that the perlocutionary meaning (the effect on or reaction of the reader) can be as determinative as those meanings that are locutionary (concerned with the act of saying) or illocutionary (concerned with the act of doing).

How, then, does perlocutionary meaning work specifically in this excerpt from Pagnol? Even though some of the syntactic impact is lost in the translation from the original French, this excerpt, most of it from contiguous paragraphs, illustrates the way that stylistic effects exist in stretches of discourse beyond sentences. The real impact, in fact, lies in the way Pagnol, after carefully presenting other aspects of his memoir, creates a fast-forward effect and, in just a few paragraphs, encapsulates years of significant events of life and death. Each death is recounted in its propositional detail—simply as a fact of time passing—with the image of the mill-wheel a metaphor that underscores the inevitability of time and death. It is significant to note that Pagnol achieves greater emotional impact specifically by using an economy of words, or conciseness, in conjunction with amplification, which involves elaboration or copiousness. Nevin Laib (1990) calls conciseness and amplification "companion arts." He states that conciseness "focuses the mind and reflects concentration. It suggests decisiveness, maturity, and strength" (457). In this instance, conciseness is achieved not through individual words or sentences but through the economy of units of discourse beyond the sentence. Pagnol uses concision almost as a catalog of events, with the few words that mark each death evoking the idea of "less is more." The intensity of the emotional impact is thus achieved through the author's ability to focus time, death, and loss through a "compression of content" (Erasmus 1978, 300).

The idea that style gives rise to meaning that goes beyond propositional meaning also changes the way we think about memory. It is possible, in fact, that memory may be as much the emotional force created by style as it is the recollection the reader has of propositional statements. In this sense, I suggest, style produces a remnant or remainder, that is, a feeling that lingers after other aspects of the text have escaped our immediate memory—aspects like the author's meaning or the meaning we have constructed from the text itself. Marcel Proust (1981) attempted to capture this elusive quality through his evocation of the *madeleine*, a small cookie whose taste and smell evoked memories that were otherwise buried in a distant time and place. I propose, then, that style serves as a kind of madeleine, the essence of what remains of an author's writing. I argue that Pagnol, in effect, engenders this type of memory through stylistic devices, among them Laib's idea of a conjunction of conciseness and amplification. Pagnol achieves this in successive paragraphs first by amplifying the reality of the death of his mother, affiliating it with the horses and coffins, the black dress, the silence, an approach he repeats in giving salient details of his brother's death (e.g., the mouth-organ on the table) and of Lili's (e.g., the flowers, immortelles, that cover the land in which he is buried, and the irony of Lili's lack of knowledge of northern plants when he had taught the author about the vegetation of Provence). He couples this expanded language of memory with his succinct staccato-like interpretation of that memory: the inevitability of man's fate; the sadness of the human condition; the reluctance to share that knowledge with children. Thus, the connection of conciseness and amplification in successive units of discourse beyond the sentence, referring back to the entire two-volume memoir, suggests that memory can be recalled, and focused, through stylistic resources.

RECOVERING HISTORY

If it is true that part of our attitude toward the study of style today is based on a misunderstanding of its history in our field, why is that significant? I have argued that our disavowal of stylistic practices has deprived the field of many useful language resources in the teaching of writing: not only such teaching practices as syntactically based generative rhetoric and sentence combining, but also features of language like sound and rhythm; vocabulary and diction; cohesion, coherence, and variation in sentence types (loose, periodic, balanced, etc.); questions of rhetorical usage, rhetorical grammar, and rhetorical imitation; and the given and new contract, punctuation, and spelling. These stylistic interests, which represent just a small sample of the overall possibilities, coincide with a period of the field's history identified not only as the process era (the Golden Age of style), but also the beginning of modern composition studies. Thus, in our neglect of these interests, we also ignore a part of our roots, including disciplinary ties to the revival of rhetoric and an interest in science (e.g., cognitive theories). Therefore, the reanimation of stylistic study contributes to reformulating the history of that period and, by extension, the history of our discipline. It forces us to ask whether we want the study of style to remain hermetically sealed even after we have begun to reconstruct some of the reasons for its isolation, and concomitant dispersion, in the field.

In any attempt to recover the history of the process era, it is important to think about the way that era has been constructed retrospectively. Bruce Horner reminds us of this point in his essay "Resisting Traditions in Composing Composition," where he writes that "advice on the 'search' for traditions leaves unchallenged a tacit conception of traditions as inert objects, hidden but nonetheless discoverable by those with the requisite time, access to materials, and sensibility. Overlooked is the *process* by which traditions in composition are constituted and maintained" (Horner 1994, 495; emphasis added). The problem is that the process era has itself undergone an interpretive process in which rhetorical features of style have been constructed as inert objects, and composition scholars have accepted that process without questioning the discipline's "final word" on the tradition. For instance, in their afterword to the volume *Teaching/Writing in the Late Age of Print* (Galin, Haviland, and Johnson 2003), the editors suggest that one instructor's "social-minded" classroom teaching is actually informed by "tenets of current-traditional . . . rhetorics" (385) and cite as evidence the instructor's use of the words "genre," "research," "style," and "tone" in her syllabus (386). The editors' search for evidence of a pejorative current-traditional paradigm among other social features that the instructor uses rhetorically and dynamically suggests their reliance on what Horner calls an inert tradition. Clearly, this is an inaccurate tradition—and interpretation—perpetuated by a process that has gone unchallenged, and in its place I am proposing a revisionist history of the period with respect to style.

One way to reexamine traditions and to question some of the process movement's assumptions is to reread composition scholars who participated in that era. In that regard, I propose to revisit the work of scholars who are not normally associated with style, and two potential choices are Peter Elbow, most often associated with expressivism, and James Britton, thought to have made an important distinction between poetic and transactional knowledge. In the same way that Horner (1994) rereads the work of William E. Coles, Jr. and David Bartholomae and their reception in composition studies, I suggest a rereading of figures like Elbow and Britton and, in the process, as Horner proposes, "critiquing common identifications of their work with particular traditions and arguing for an alternative identification of their work" (497)—in this case, in the stylistic tradition. What were the operative concepts and traditions that each worked from and how can those traditions be reconciled with different views of style during that era? From what perspectives and on what terms would such a rethinking of their work occur? How did these views enter their pedagogies? The aim, then, is to examine precisely how their work is suggestive of style when, in fact, it is generally thought not to be about style at all. I have mentioned a few of the figures in composition who were central to the process era; there are many others. For example, two scholars more closely affiliated with the study of style during the Golden Age, Ross Winterowd and Richard Young, are worthy of study. I propose, then, a broad-based reassessment of individuals during the Golden Age and an examination of how their work might be reread through the lens of style.

In addition, it would be productive to reexamine the study of style through composition's rich textbook tradition, particularly during the process era. Some of the textbooks that would serve as a place to start include Young, Becker, and Pike's (1970) *Rhetoric: Discovery and Change,* which has a rich but largely unknown section on style; Ann Berthoff's (1982) *Forming/Thinking/Writing*, which has important things to say about imitation and focuses its work, as a general rule, at the word and sentence level; Patrick Hartwell's (1982) *Open to Language*, with several chapters on style and other language features; Edward P. J. Corbett's (1971) *Classical Rhetoric for the Modern Student*, with its series of rhetorical exercises and readings on style; and one of the five editions of Daiker, Kerek, Morenberg, and Sommers's (1994) *The Writer's Options: Lessons in Style and Arrangement*, organized around the idea of sentence combining and extended into various areas of composition. One question to ask is how textbook practices reflect the scholarship going on at the time and how they perpetuate views about style that support or contradict those views. To what extent are these textbooks indicative of efforts on multiple levels to use style to generate language? In what ways do they confirm or contradict some of the practices labeled "current-traditional" by the critics of the time? How do the textbooks accept or resist popular conceptions of style regarding clarity or grammar (see Chap. 5)? For example, Berthoff's text is often thought of as creating a new space for thinking about language. In what ways might she be working against her own formulation of new thinking? In other words, how does *Forming/Thinking/Writing* reflect or resist conventional notions of style and invention?

EXPLORING THE DIASPORA

I have argued that style, despite its apparent invisibility, has migrated to various areas of the field where it is not called style but functions as such under different theories and practices. I have given examples in genre theory, rhetorical analysis, personal writing, and studies of race, class, gender, and cultural difference. These are not the only areas of composition's diaspora, however, and it would be productive to explore other spaces where the study of style has migrated in the field. Some of these include studies of literacy, including multiliteracies, technology, and globalization. In addition to examining the way in which style has diffused in these areas of composition, it is important to draw on the disciplines that inform them. For example, if we look at the innovative area of multiliteracies, we discover that the study of style is having an impact there in important ways, sometimes identified as style and sometimes not called style but functioning in that way (e.g., the idea of "design"). It is important to note, too, that the pedagogy of multiliteracies does not function alone but takes as its assumption the challenges of a global world and advances in technology, both of which invoke the canon of style in innovative ways. Collin Brooke (2002) points to this problem in an article in *Enculturation*, "Notes toward the Remediation of Style," where he introduces the importance of style as "remediation," defined by Jay David Bolter and Richard Grusin (1999) as "the representation of one medium in another" (45). Brooke suggests a view of a style remediated through new technologies in a globalized world. Drawing on the work of Lanham (1993), Brooke states that "one of the implications of electronic prose is that style escapes the cage that print technology represents."

The importance of globalization, including the impact of technology, is evident in all aspects of composition studies today. For example, in the afterword of *Teaching/Writing in the Late Age of Print*, editors Galin, Haviland, and Johnson (2003) consider the implications of globalism for composition:

> Our discipline faces now daunting responsibilities as post-modernism is pressed by globalism on both theoretical and material planes. This confluence of diversifying and unifying cultural forces confronts us on theoretical planes when aims and praxis collide. For example, we have begun to theorize alternative texts and invite our students to write them; yet we are faced with increasing pressures to prepare our students for the global corporate workplace. . . . Faculty can teach themselves and their students to consider seriously the multiple ways texts can be composed and read, working to "illuminate rather than mask" the possibilities emerging from cultural and other differences. (403)

In their emphasis on a diversity of texts composed and read on the basis of "difference," the editors are essentially calling for the very kind of alternatives proposed in "Students' Right to Their Own Language" (Committee on CCCC Language 1974). The Students' Right authors recognize the study of style as part of composition's disciplinary responsibility, and the editors of *Teaching/Writing* seem to come close to the idea of style as part of global interdependence when they suggest the "confluence of diversifying and unifying cultural forces . . . [where] aims and praxis collide" (403).

Whereas the editors of *Teaching/Writing* stop short of explicitly including style in their vision of composition in a globalized world, Bill Cope and Mary Kalantzis (2000), the editors of *Multiliteracies: Literacy, Learning, and the Design of Social Futures,* make it an indispensable part of their project. Like the editors of *Teaching/Writing,* who look for ways to increase both local diversity and global connectedness, *Multiliteracies* editors argue that "the proximity of cultural and linguistic diversity is one of the key facts of our time" (6). Yet, the *Multiliteracies* writers propose to enter global diversity by means of a key concept: "Design." The authors define Design as a way to "conceptualise the 'what' of literacy pedagogy":

> The key concept we developed to do this is that of Design, in which we are both inheritors of patterns and conventions of meaning while at the same time active designers of meaning. And, as designers of meaning, we are designers of social futures—workplace futures, public futures, and community futures. (7)

I propose that the authors' idea of Design is a rhetorical concept very much in line with what I have been describing in terms of style. In explaining the social idea of Design, the collective authors of The New London Group write, "We propose a metalanguage of Multiliteracies based on the concept of 'Design'" (19), and go on to define that metalanguage:

> Design is intended to focus our attention on representational resources. This metalanguage is not a category of mechanical skills,

> as is commonly the case in grammars designed for educational use. Nor is it the basis for detached critique or reflection. Rather, *the Design notion emphasizes the productive and innovative potential of language as a meaning-making system.* This is an action-oriented and generative description of language as a means of representation. (25–26; emphasis added)

I contend that the authors' conception of Design is similar to the definition of style I have explored in this book. Just as I have argued that style has often been used for productive and creative purposes, the *Multiliteracies* authors suggest that design emphasizes "the productive and innovative potential of language as a meaning-making system" (26).

It seems, then, that the authors have essentially redefined style as Design. In doing so, they have also proposed a possible way to overcome the form/content dichotomy that has been so much at the heart of the disciplinary division about style for years. The New London Group hints at this resolution when they write:

> The notion of design connects powerfully to the sort of creative intelligence the best practitioners need in order to be able continually to redesign their activities in the very act of practice. It connects well to the idea that learning and productivity are the results of the designs . . . of complex systems of people environments, technology, beliefs, and texts. (19–20)

In the eyes of the *Multiliteracies* authors, Design is necessarily a combination of form and content because the two are connected in an ongoing process of renegotiation and redesign. While looking at various systems of meaning like people, technology, and texts, the authors recognize that language is a productive and innovative way of making meaning through representation. It is clear, then, that language is a fundamental part of any Design activity—any feature of style—according to the New London Group authors.

In addition to looking to such areas of style's migration as the concept of Design, it is important to reconsider the vexed term of the "diaspora" (see Chap. 4). Janice Lauer did not explicitly intend the concept to connote a forced migration into other areas of the discipline, yet that notion seems appropriate in terms of the marginalization of style in composition studies. In other arenas, the field of composition has tried to use its position at the margins to wage a number of battles involving, for instance, the role of contingent labor, issues of gender equity, and the effort to be recognized as a discipline separate from traditional English studies, with its focus on literature and cultural studies. It seems, however, that what was at one time a forced migration of style might now be more accurately described as a self-imposed exile. This is unfortunate for many reasons, including the missed opportunity for a rapprochement that the study of style offers.

The understanding of style I have presented encompasses both writing (invention) and reading (stylistic analysis). In the past, these different views have been emblematic of the "great divide" of composition and literature and the split in English departments (see Tokarczyk and Papoulis 2003). I propose that the study of style is one way to bridge that divide. In line with this thinking, it seems that style could be resurrected from its exile to provide leadership in the debates surrounding the so-called great divide. The unique aspect of this possibility is the leadership the field of composition would provide through its expertise in the study of style to demonstrate the productive nature of stylistic resources for both writing and reading. What would it take for members of the discipline to acknowledge our debt to style in its current scholarship?

CREATING A PUBLIC HISTORY

Along with what today must be viewed as the self-imposed exile of style in composition, I argue that as a field, we have given up opportunities that involve expectations from those outside the field. Regardless of how much compositionists may object, composition as a field is expected to claim a certain degree of expertise in style studies and other areas of language, sometimes extending to grammar. Because of our ambivalence toward these areas of expertise, however, there has been an unexpected consequence: we have been precluded from having a legitimate voice in other areas of concern to the field. For example, crucial issues involving literacy (e.g., recent questions about computer-based scoring of writing exams), standardized testing, and movements by college campuses to shift writing courses out of writing programs or English departments and place them in schools of business or elsewhere are constantly confronting the field. I argue, however, that we do not have a great deal of credibility in these areas partly because of our reluctance to deal with issues of style. For that reason, I assert that composition itself should produce its own version of the public intellectual, a suggestion that Frank Farmer intimates in his work, urging that the concept be redefined as the "community intellectual." When is the last time that one of our scholars appeared as a critic or columnist in the *New Yorker*, writing a freelance piece for the *Atlantic*, or sending in an op-ed column for the *New York Times* or *Washington Post*? What is stopping us as a field from developing a more visible public presence?[1]

The failure to address stylistic practices as part of our disciplinary theory and pedagogy and to have a public voice about those issues has had the unwitting effect of bringing about a kind of invisibility in the profession. As recent work has shown, the study of style and style-related issues has moved into the public sphere, where it has been the source of tremendous interest and frequent debate. That debate has been controlled, however, by a group poised to project their views of style onto the public. As Edward Finegan (1980) has shown through his study of two controversies over language in the 1960s, public conceptions tend to express absolutist views at odds with the relativistic views the field of composition (and experts in other fields) have adopted. Nonetheless, in the absence of a willingness to take up style studies, composition is left without any response except to disagree. And who is listening? Indeed, it seems we would be hard-pressed to name many composition-trained experts who have weighed in when significant issues involving the field are raised in the public sphere. If we want to be heard in areas that our research and history have prepared us to lead in, composition needs to take back the study of style. Indeed, as articles in public discourse make clear, stylistic issues often overlap with questions of literacy, grammar, and other subjects in which the public at large has a recurring interest.

I am not suggesting that the discipline simply return to looking at style in the way scholars did in the 1970s and 1980s, or thoughtlessly adopt, for instance, the use of classical tropes and schemes in the classroom. I am proposing rather that compositionists redefine style in a way that is meaningful to the field and that makes the study of style consonant with our disciplinary vision. Clearly, we can get some guidance from the stylistic practices that have been used in the past. In addition, I have tried to suggest areas outside the field where promising work is being done that impacts the study of style. One of the most fertile resources exists in composition's own backyard, that is, in areas where the stylistic traditions and practices have migrated. How can those areas, through a reverse analytical process, give us an idea of the types of stylistic practices and techniques that would be most useful for scholars and teachers of composition? One possibility is to examine how some of the work applies to areas outside composition. For example, in her recent book *College Writing and Beyond: A New Framework for University Writing Instruction*, Anne Beaufort (2007) suggests that in learning to write history, one critical aspect of subject matter expertise "is the ability to do critical thinking appropriate to the discipline—specifically, in history, to see similarities and differences across source documents and to apply a critical framework to a particular text, seeing connections or disjunctures" (79). It would be useful to consider composition's critical frameworks in writing in interdisciplinary areas.

In that light, one place we might look for guidance is Susan Jarratt's (2003) *Enculturation* piece, "Rhetoric in Crisis?: The View from Here." In response to a question posed by the journal editors about whether rhetoric is in a crisis state in composition, "left behind" with scholars in the field "'over' rhetoric like a fleeting relationship," Jarratt responds by saying "no," arguing that "rhetoric continues to thrive in several corners of academic and public space." In looking to the public sphere, Jarratt proposes first that evidence of the importance of rhetoric can be found in a significant number of articles published about the war in Iraq by the popular press. She also finds evidence for hope in the number of new books about rhetoric published by university presses, some of which have competed for a new Rhetoric Society of America book award. Jarratt goes on to cite the second edition of the MLA's *Introduction to Scholarship in Modern Languages and Literatures,* which includes two separate essays on "rhetoric" and "composition," a change from the first edition in which the two words were combined. She also sees the formation of a new "meta-organization," the Alliance of Rhetoric Societies, as promising. As counterevidence, Jarratt suggests the general tendency among the public and academic colleagues not to recognize rhetoric as an academic specialty; the recent publication of a book, *The Ends of Rhetoric,* with no mention of the discipline of rhetoric and composition; and the presence of only eight full-time faculty in rhetoric and composition in the University of California system in which Jarratt works, whose total faculty exceeds 5,000 members.

This article is important because it gives a way to evaluate the crisis of style in the profession. While Jarratt concludes that rhetoric is not in crisis, it would be difficult to make the same assessment of the state of style studies, especially when style has been isolated from its natural companions in rhetoric. According to Jarratt, rhetoric continues to thrive in several areas of the public sphere, a claim I have also made about style. Jarratt does not see any conflict between public and academic presentations of rhetoric, while I have highlighted that conflict with respect to style. Clearly, the notion of style that gets carried forth into the public sphere is not often the one we hold in the field. Still, it would be instructive to look for other evidence of style in the public sphere to see the various ways in which it is conceived and to search for areas of rapprochement.

In following Jarratt's example, it would also be useful to look for additional evidence of publications about style in the field. I have mentioned a few recent articles in some of the prominent journals in composition. T. R. Johnson and Thomas Pace (2005) edited the published collection *Refiguring Prose Style*. Despite this small progress, however, publications about style are virtually absent from composition studies and cannot begin to compare with the academic publications on rhetoric cited by Jarratt. It would be useful nonetheless to see if writing about style has been buried in unusual places or if, as I have asserted, there are other sites of the diaspora that could be explored. In terms of institutional practices, which Jarratt finds both abundant and lacking for rhetoric, it would be useful to look to websites for evidence of the state of style in various writing curricula across the country. Where is style being taught, in what ways, using what texts? How is it being defined? A survey of scholars in the field, perhaps on the WPA listserv, could also yield productive results.

Unlike Jarratt's investigation of rhetoric, I do not expect the search for evidence of style to turn up much in the academy, though admittedly, interest in style has been extensive in the public sphere. Jarratt assesses the crisis in rhetoric. In order for a crisis to exist, however, there has to be enough of an exigency for people to believe there's a problem. In the case of style in composition studies, its absence, invisibility, and neglect have not as of yet engendered the type of response that prompted the special issue of *Enculturation* on rhetoric in crisis. I hope this book demonstrates that there is, in fact, a crisis of style in composition and rhetoric. Yet, with some give-and-take between the public and academic spheres, among composition scholars, and perhaps in dialogue with other professions, the study of style could once again be a legitimate area of theory and practice in the field.

NOTES

CHAPTER 1

1. Williams's analysis is part of a fine collection of articles in *Written Communication* about a pedagogical essay on writing style written by Bakhtin in 1945, "Dialogic Origin and Dialogic Pedagogy of Grammar: Stylistics as Part of Russian Language Instruction in Secondary School." Charles Bazerman gives an excellent summary of the recently translated essay for the journal. It begins: "Without constantly considering the stylistic significance of grammatical choices, the instruction of grammar inevitably turns into scholasticism. In practice, however, the instructor very rarely provides any sort of stylistic interpretation of the grammatical forms covered in class" (334). Bahktin proceeds to offer his analysis of the virtues of a paratactic style, virtually absent from his students' writing before he begins instruction, and a hypotactic style that students find "colder, drier, and more logical" (335). The volume includes individual responses to Bakhtin's essay by Frank Farmer, Joseph M. Williams, and Kay Halasek, followed by further responses in which the authors respond to each other. Bazerman ends by suggesting that Bakhtin, ostensibly like most teachers, struggles with "how to maintain the freshness, uniqueness, and local responsiveness of utterances, even as we provide students more sophisticated tools of analysis and reflective choice making" (371).
2. While the "public turn" in composition studies arguably occurred several years ago, Mathieu (2005) is the first person to coin the term in her book *Tactics of Hope*, subtitled *The Public Turn in English Composition.* Mathieu suggests that the public turn involves "a desire for writing to enter civic debates; for street life to enter classrooms through a focus on local, social issues; for students to hit the streets by performing service, and for teachers and scholars to conduct activist or community-grounded research" (1–2).

CHAPTER 2

1. This chapter, which argues that there is a tension throughout stylistic history in terms of virtues of style and levels of style, is not intended to chronicle the history of style or to be an exhaustive survey. Indeed, it would be impossible to undertake such a task within the limits of a chapter tailored specifically to the issues I address in the rest of the book. Instead, I focus primarily on relevant theories of style in classical rhetoric and Renaissance rhetoric before moving to contemporary theories and issues of style. While my approach is chronological, it is necessarily selective. For example, I omitted a section on Medieval rhetors because I did not find their work to be as relevant to the argument in my book as those from other historical periods.

CHAPTER 3

1. Pace's use of the term "renaissance" is apt, and I adopt it to describe the flourishing of style studies during the Golden Age of style. Pace investigates the stylistic options provided by Francis Christensen, Edward P. J. Corbett, and Winston Weathers and interprets them as a way to improve students' rhetorical success in composition pedagogy.
2. Johnson's book is highly readable and engaging and offers a useful appendix of "stylistic principles and devices." In his appendix, Johnson reproduces his instructions to students: "When you revise your papers, I want you to think very deliberately about eight different stylistic principles: transition, clarity, emphasis, balance, figurative language, syntax, restatement, and sound. These principles have been identified by Robert Harris as essential elements of style" (99).

CHAPTER 4

1. Jim Zebroski's *JAC* article, "Theory in the Diaspora," points in useful ways to the plight of theory in the field and suggests that "theory, theories, and sometimes theorists are moving around, dispersing to a wider range of sites in and out of rhetoric and composition, no less pervasive or powerful for all that movement—though at times theory is harder to see and hear than it was in the late 1980s and early 1990s" (664).
2. While the idea of a diaspora in composition studies is relatively new, it seems to be a promising theoretical concept that could enable the field to make overtures to other disciplines in order to see where other areas that the field has abandoned have migrated. In addition to the areas of style and invention, for instance, it seems that a case could be made for exploring the dispersion of interest in arrangement and delivery.

CHAPTER 5

1. The journal *The Public Interest* ceased publication with its Spring 2005 issue, after 40 years. The founding editor Irving Kristol suggested that the journal did not have a particular ideology, but most would describe the journal as conservative or "neo-conservative," and it's clear that Mac Donald's article presents a view of composition studies that is far from balanced.
2. Warner's view of clarity is highly relevant to composition and rhetoric. He asks, for instance, "What kind of clarity is necessary in writing?" After stating the conventional wisdom that "writing that is unclear to nonspecialists is just 'bad writing,'" Warner goes on to make an argument relevant to compositionists writing in the public sphere: "People who share this view will be generally reluctant to concede that different kinds of writing suit different purposes, that what is clear in one reading community will be unclear in another, that clarity depends on shared conventions and common references, that one man's jargon is another's clarity, that perceptions of jargon or unclarity change over time" (138).

CHAPTER 6

1. The Council of Writing Program Administrators (WPA's) Network for Media Action has begun to address this problem. According to the group's Web site, "The WPA-NMA both monitors mainstream media for examples of these stories [e.g., about first-year writing, the SAT, and plagiarism], and provides tips on how to begin entering the conversation about them on your campus and/or in your community." See http://www.wpacouncil.org/nma.

REFERENCES

Abbott, Don Paul. 2001. Rhetoric and Writing in the Renaissance. In Murphy 2001, 145–72.

Althusser, Louis. 1971. Ideology and Ideological State Apparatuses: Notes Toward an Investigation. *Lenin and Philosophy and Other Essays. Part 2.* Trans. Ben Brewster. New York: Monthly Review. 127–88.

Anson, Chris M., Robert A. Schwegler, and Marcia F. Muth. 2003. *The Longman Writer's Companion.* 2nd ed. New York: Longman.

Aristotle. 1954. *Rhetoric* and *Poetics.* Trans. W. Rhys Roberts. New York: Modern Library/Random House.

———. 1991. *On Rhetoric: A Theory of Civic Discourse.* Trans. George A. Kennedy. New York: Oxford Univ. Press.

Atwill, Janet M., and Janice M. Lauer, eds. 2002. *Perspectives on Rhetorical Invention. Tennessee Studies in Literature* 39. Knoxville: Univ. of Tennessee Press.

Bakhtin, Mikhail. 1981. *The Dialogic Imagination: Four Essays.* Ed. Michael Holquist. Trans. Caryl Emerson and Michael Holquist. Austin: Univ. of Texas Press.

Barthes, Roland. 1971. Style and Its Image. In Chatman 1971, 3–10.

Bateman, Donald R., and Frank J. Zidonis. 1964. *The Effect of a Knowledge of Generative Grammar upon the Growth of Language Complexity.* Columbus: The Ohio State Univ. Press.

Bateman, Donald, and Frank Zidonis, eds. 1970. *A Grammatico-Semantic Explanation of the Problems of Sentence Formation and Interpretations in the Classroom. Vols. I and II.* Columbus, OH: The Ohio State Research Foundation with the U.S. Department of Health, Education, and Welfare.

Bawarshi, Anis S. 2003. *Genre and the Invention of the Writer: Reconsidering the Place of Invention in Composition.* Logan: Utah State Univ. Press.

Bazerman, Charles. 2005. An Essay on Pedagogy by Mikhail M. Bakhtin. *Written Communication* 22: 333–38.

Bazerman, Charles, Frank Farmer, Kay Halasek, and Joseph M. Williams. 2005. Responses to Bakhtin's "Dialogic Origins and Dialogic Pedagogy of Grammar: Stylistics as Part of Russian Language Instruction in Secondary Schools": Further Responses and a Tentative Conclusion. *Written Communication* 22: 363–74.

Beardsley, Monroe C. 1967. In Steinmann 1967, 192–213.

Beaufort, Anne. 2007. *College Writing and Beyond: A New Framework for University Writing Instruction.* Logan: Utah State Univ. Press.

Beggs, James S. 1984. The Role of Spelling in Composition for Older Students. In Moran and Lunsford 1984, 319–46.

Behar, Ruth. 1993. *Translated Woman: Crossing the Border with Esperanza's Story.* Boston: Beacon.

———. 1995. Writing in My Father's Name: A Diary of *Translated Woman's* First Year. In *Women Writing Culture.* Ed. Ruth Behar and Deborah A. Gordon, 65–82. Berkeley: Univ. of California Press.

Benveniste, Emile. 1971. *Problems in General Linguistics.* Trans. Mary Elizabeth Meek. Coral Gables, FL: Univ. of Miami Press.

Berlin, James A. 1987. *Rhetoric and Reality: Writing Instruction in American Colleges, 1900–1985.* Carbondale: Southern Illinois Univ. Press.

Berlin, James A., and Robert P. Inkster. 1980. Current-Traditional Rhetoric: Paradigm and Practice. *Freshman English News* 8: 1–4, 13–14.

Bernstein, Basil. 1964. Elaborated and Restricted Codes: Their Social Origins and Some Consequences. *American Anthropologist* 66.6 (Part 2): 55–69.

Berthoff, Ann E. 1981. *The Making of Meaning: Metaphors, Models, and Maxims for Writing Teachers.* Portsmouth, NH: Heinemann-Boynton/Cook.

———. 1982. *Forming/Thinking/Writing: The Composing Imagination.* Portsmouth, NH: Heinemann-Boynton/Cook.

Bishop, Wendy. 1997. Alternate Styles for Who, What, and Why? Some Introductions to *Elements of Alternate Style: Essays on Writing and Revision* (Including an E-Mail Interview with Winston Weathers). In Bishop 1997, 3–9.

———, ed. 1997. *Elements of Alternate Style: Essays on Writing and Revision.* Portsmouth, NH: Heinemann-Boynton/Cook.

Bizzell, Patricia, and Bruce Herzberg. 2001. *The Rhetorical Tradition: Readings from Classical Times to the Present.* 2nd ed. Boston: Bedford/St. Martin's.

Black, Laurel Johnson. 1995. Stupid Rich Bastards. In *This Fine Place So Far from Home: Voices of Academics from the Working Class.* Ed. C.L. Barney Dews and Carolyn Leste Law, 13–25. Philadelphia: Temple Univ. Press.

Blakesley, David. 1995. Reconceptualizing Grammar as an Aspect of Rhetorical Invention. In *The Place of Grammar in Writing Instruction.* Ed. Susan Hunter and Ray Wallace, 191–203. Portsmouth, NH: Boynton/Cook.

Bleich, David, and Deborah H. Holdstein. 2001. Introduction: Recognizing the Human in the Humanities. In *Personal Effects: The Social Character of Scholarly Writing.* Ed. Deborah H. Holdstein and David Bleich, 1–24. Logan: Utah State Univ. Press.

Bolter, Jay David, and Richard Grusin. 1999. *Remediation: Understanding New Media.* Cambridge, MA: MIT.

Braddock, Richard, Richard Lloyd-Jones, and Lowell Schoer. 1963. *Research in Written Composition.* Urbana, IL: NCTE.

Brandt, Deborah, letter to the editor, *New York Times,* May 31, 2005.

Brooke, Collin. 2002. Perspective: Notes toward the Remediation of Style. *Enculturation Special Multi-Journal Issue on Electronic Publication* 4.1 (Spring). http://enculturation.gmu.edu/4_1/style (accessed March 1, 2007)

Brooks, Phyllis. 1973. Mimesis: Grammar and the Echoing Voice. *College English* 35: 161–68.

Burke, Kenneth. 1941. *The Philosophy of Literary Form: Studies in Symbolic Action.* New York: Vintage/Random House.

———. 1968. *Counter-Statement.* 2nd ed. Berkeley: Univ. of California Press.

Carbone, Nick. 2004. War Against Grammar. WPA-L, February 25, 2004, https://lists.asu.edu/cgi-bin/wa?A2=ind0402&L=WPA-L&P=R55807&D=0&H=0&O=T&T=1

Chafe, Wallace L. 1973. Language and Memory. *Lang* 49: 261–81.

Chatman, Seymour, ed. and trans. 1971. *Literary Style: A Symposium.* London: Oxford Univ. Press.

Ching, Marvin K. L. 1984. Usage. In Moran and Lunsford 1984, 399–424.

Chomsky, Noam. 1957. *Syntactic Structures.* The Hague: Mouton.

———. 1965. *Aspects of the Theory of Syntax.* Cambridge, MA: The MIT Press.

Christensen, Francis. 1963 A Generative Rhetoric of the Sentence. *College Composition and Communication* 14: 155–67.

Christensen, Francis, and Bonnijean Christensen. 1978. *Notes toward a New Rhetoric: Nine Essays for Teachers.* 2nd ed. New York: Harper & Row.

Cicero. 1939. *Brutus.* Trans. G. L. Hendrickson. Cambridge, MA: Harvard Univ. Press. 19–293.

———. 1939. *Orator.* Trans. H. M. Hubbell. Cambridge, MA: Harvard Univ. Press. 306–509.

———. 1959. *De Oratore.* Trans. E. W. Sutton. Vol. 1, bk. 1, 2. Cambridge, MA: Harvard Univ. Press.

———. 1960. *De Oratore.* Trans. H. Rackham. Vol. 2, bk. 3. Cambridge, MA: Harvard Univ. Press.

Cmiel, Kenneth. 1990. *Democratic Eloquence: The Fight over Popular Speech in Nineteenth-Century America.* New York: William Morrow.

Coe, Richard M., 1987. An Apology for Form; or, Who Took the Form Out of the Process? *College English* 49: 13–28.

———. Generative Rhetoric. 1998. In Kennedy 1998, 131–36.

Committee on CCCC Language. 1974. Students' Right to Their Own Language. *College Composition and Communication* 25: 1–18.

Connors, Robert J. 1981. The Rise and Fall of the Modes of Discourse. *College Composition and Communication* 32: 444–55.

———. 1997. *Composition-Rhetoric: Backgrounds, Theory, and Pedagogy.* Pittsburgh: Univ. of Pittsburgh Press.

———. 2000. The Erasure of the Sentence. *College Composition and Communication* 52: 96–128.

———, ed. 1989. *Selected Essays of Edward P. J. Corbett.* Dallas: Southern Methodist Univ. Press.

Connors, Robert J., and Cheryl Glenn. 1999. *The New St. Martin's Guide to Teaching Writing.* Boston: Bedford/St. Martin's.

Cope, Bill, and Mary Kalantzis, eds. 2000. *Multiliteracies: Literacy Learning and the Design of Social Futures.* For the New London Group. London: Routledge/Taylor & Francis.

Corbett, Edward P. J. 1971. *Classical Rhetoric for the Modern Student.* 2nd ed. New York: Oxford Univ. Press.

———. 1976. Approaches to the Study of Style. In Tate 1976, 73–109.

———. 1981. A Method of Analyzing Prose Style with a Demonstration Analysis of Swift's *A Modest Proposal.* In *The Writing Teacher's Sourcebook.* Ed. Gary Tate and Edward P. J. Corbett, 333–52. New York: Oxford Univ. Press.

———.1986. Teaching Style. In McQuade 1986, 23–33.

———. 1989a. A Survey of Rhetoric from *Classical Rhetoric for the Modern Student, 1971.* In Connors 1989, 114–76.

———. 1989b. The Theory and Practice of Imitation in Classical Rhetoric, 1971. In Connors 1989, 177–91.

Crowley, Sharon. 1989. Linguistics and Composition Instruction: 1950–1980. *Written Communication* 6: 480–505.

———. 1990. *The Methodical Memory: Invention in Current-Traditional Rhetoric.* Carbondale: Southern Illinois Univ. Press.

Crowley, Sharon, and Debra Hawhee. 2004. *Ancient Rhetorics for Contemporary Students.* 3rd ed. New York: Pearson/Longman.

Daiker, Donald A., Andrew Kerek, and Max Morenberg. 1978. Sentence-Combining and Syntactic Maturity in Freshman English. *College Composition and Communication* 29: 36–41.

———, eds. 1979. *Sentence Combining and the Teaching of Writing.* Akron, OH: Univ. of Akron.

———, eds. 1985. *Sentence-Combining: A Rhetorical Perspective.* Carbondale: Southern Illinois Univ. Press.

Daiker, Donald A., Andrew Kerek, Max Morenberg, and Jeffrey Sommers. 1994. *The Writer's Options: Combining to Composing.* 5th ed. New York: Harper Collins College.

D'Alton, J. F. 1962. *Roman Literary Theory and Criticism: A Study in Tendencies.* New York: Russell and Russell.

Daneš, Frantisek, ed. 1974. *Papers on Functional Sentence Perspective.* The Hague: Mouton.

D'Angelo, Frank. 1976. Notes toward a Semantic Theory of Rhetoric within a Case Grammar Framework. *College Composition and Communication* 28: 359–62.

Davis, Robert Con. 1987. Freud's Resistance to Reading and Teaching. Psychoanalysis and Pedagogy I. *College English* 49: 621–27.

de Heredia, José-María. 1978. The Conquistadores. In *Trophées. Trophies, with Other Sonnets.* Westport, CT: Hyperion. 117.

Demetrius. *On Style.* 1932. Trans. W. Rhys Roberts. Cambridge, MA: Harvard Univ. Press.

de Vise, Daniel. 2006. Clauses and Commas Make a Comeback: SAT Helps Return Grammar to Class. *Washington Post* 23 Oct. 2006: A1. http://www.Washingtonpost.com/wp–dyn/content/article/2006/10/22/AR2006102201135.html (accessed 30 May 2007).

Devitt, Amy J. 1997. Genre as Language Standard. In *Genre and Writing: Issues, Arguments, Alternatives.* Ed. Wendy Bishop and Hans Ostrom, 45–55. Portsmouth, NH: Boynton/Cook.

Dillon, George L. 1981. *Constructing Texts: Elements of a Theory of Composition and Style.* Bloomington: Indiana Univ. Press.

Duncan, Mike. 2007. Whatever Happened to the Paragraph? *College English* 69: 470–95.

Edwards, Bruce L. 1996. Tagmemics. In T. Enos, 1996. 715–18.

Elbow, Peter. 1985. The Challenge for Sentence Combining. In Daiker, Kerek, and Morenberg 1985, 232–45.

———. 2002. The Cultures of Literature and Composition. *College English* 64: 533–46.

Enkvist, Nils Erik. 1964. On Defining Style: An Essay in Applied Linguistics. In *Linguistics and Style.* Ed. Nils Erik Enkvist, John Spencer, and Michael J. Gregory, 3–56. London: Oxford Univ. Press.

———. 1971. On the Place of Style in Some Linguistic Theories. In Chatman 1971, 47–64.

Enos, Richard Leo. 2001. Ancient Greek Writing Instruction. In Murphy 2001, 9–34.

———. 2004. The Art of Rhetoric at Rhodes: An Eastern Rival to the Athenian Representation of Classical Rhetoric. In *Rhetoric before and beyond the Greeks.* Ed. Carol S. Lipson and Roberta A, Binkley, 183–96. Albany: State Univ. of New York Press.

Enos, Theresa, ed. 1996. *The Encyclopedia of Rhetoric and Composition: Communication from Ancient Times to the Information Age.* New York: Garland.

Erasmus, Desiderius. 1978. Copia: Foundations of the Abundant Style. Trans. Betty I. Knott. In *Collected Works of Erasmus.* Ed. Craig R. Thompson. Vol. 24. Toronto: Univ. of Toronto Press. Quoted in Bizzell and Herzberg 2001.

Fahnestock, Jeanne, and Marie Secor. 2002. Rhetorical Analysis. In *Discourse Studies in Composition.* Ed. Ellen Barton and Gail Stygall, 177–200. Creskill, NJ: Hampton.

Fahy, Francis L., letter to the editor, *New York Times,* June 3, 2005.

Farmer, Frank. 2002. Review: Community Intellectuals. *College English* 65: 202–10.

———. 2005. On Style and Other Unremarkable Things. *Written Communication* 22: 339–46.

Farmer, Frank M., and Phillip K. Arrington. 1993. Apologies and Accommodations: Imitation and the Writing Process. *Rhetoric Society Quarterly* 23: 12–34.

Finegan, Edward. 1980. *Attitudes toward English Usage: The History of a War of Words.* New York: Teachers College Press.

Fish, Stanley. 1980. Interpreting "Interpreting the Variorum." In *Is There a Text in This Class? The Authority of Interpretive Communities.* Cambridge, MA: Harvard UP. 174–80.

———. 1995. *Professional Correctness: Literary Studies and Political Change.* New York: Clarendon.

———. 1996. Professor Sokal's Bad Joke. *The New York Times* 21 May 1996: A26.

———. 2002. Say It Ain't So. *The Chronicle of Higher Education.* June 21, 2002. http://www.chronicle.com/job/2002/06/2002062101c.htm (accessed April 21, 2007.)

———. 2005. Devoid of Content. *New York Times,* May 31, 2005. http://www.nytimes.com/ 2005/05/31/opinion/31fish.html?ex=1275192000&en=5b9064f5bb67f352&ei=5090.

Flannery, Kathryn T. 1995. *The Emperor's New Clothes: Literature, Literacy, and the Ideology of Style.* Pittsburgh: Univ. of Pittsburgh Press.

Flower, Linda, and John R. Hayes. 1981. A Cognitive Process Theory of Writing. *College Composition and Communication* 39: 365–87.

Fogarty, Daniel. 1959. *Roots for a New Rhetoric.* New York: Teachers College.

Freeman, Donald C. 1970. *Linguistics and Literary Style.* New York: Holt, Rinehart and Winston.

Gage, John T. 1980. Philosophies of Style and Their Implications for Composition. *College English* 41: 615–22.

Galin, Jeff. 2005. NYTimes.com: Devoid of Content. WPA-L, 31 May 2005, https://lists.asu.edu/cgi–bin/wa?A2=ind0505&L=WPA–L&T=0&F=&S=&P=72038

Galin, Jeffrey R., Carol Peterson Haviland, and J. Paul Johnson, eds. 2003. *Teaching/Writing in the Late Age of Print.* Cresskill, NJ: Hampton.

Gere, Anne Ruggles, and Eugene Smith. 1979. *Attitudes, Language, and Change.* Urbana, IL: NCTE.

Gibson, Walker. 1966. T*ough, Sweet and Stuffy: An Essay on Modern American Prose Styles.* Bloomington: Indiana Univ. Press.

———. 1969. *Persona: A Style Study for Readers and Writers.* New York: Random House.

Gilyard, Keith. 1990. *Voices of the Self.* Detroit: Wayne State Univ. Press.

Gorgias. 1972. Encomium of Helen. In *The Older Sophists.* Ed. Rosamund Kent Sprague. Trans. George A. Kennedy. Columbia: Univ. of South Carolina Press. 50–63.

Hairston, Maxine. 1990. The Winds of Change: Thomas Kuhn and the Revolution in the Teaching of Writing. In *Rhetoric and Composition: A Sourcebook for Teachers and Writers.* 3rd. ed. Ed. Richard L. Graves. Portsmouth, NH: Heinemann-Boynton/Cook. 3–15.

Halasek, Kay. An Enriching Methodology: Bakhtin's "Dialogic Origin and Dialogic Pedagogy of Grammar" and the Teaching of Writing. *Written Communication* 22: 355–62.

Halliday, M. A. K. 1967. Notes on Transitivity and Theme in English, Part 2. *J Linguist* 3: 199–245.

Halliday, M. A. K., and Ruqaiya Hasan. 1976. *Cohesion in English.* London: Longman.

Halloran, S. Michael, and Merrill D. Whitburn. 1982. Ciceronian Rhetoric and the Rise of Science: The Plain Style Reconsidered. In *The Rhetorical Tradition and Modern Writing.* Ed. James J. Murphy. New York: MLA.

Hardin, Joe. 2004. Back to Grammar. WPA-L, March 10, 2004, https://lists.asu.edu/cgi- bin/wa?A2=ind0403&L=WPA–L&P=R17979&D=0&T=0.

Hartwell, Patrick. 1985. Grammar, Grammars, and the Teaching of Grammar. *College English* 47: 105–27.

———. *Open to Language: A New College Rhetoric.* 1982. With Robert Bentley. New York: Oxford Univ. Press.

Hawhee, Debra. 2002. Kairotic Encounters. In Atwill and Lauer 2002, 16–35.

Hendrickson, G. L. 1939. Introduction. In Cicero. *Brutus.* 2–17.

Hesse, Doug, ed. 2003. Creative Nonfiction. Special issue, *College English* 65, no.3.

Himley, Margaret. 2003. Personal Interview. 3 Apr.

Hindman, Jane E. 2001. Making Writing Matter: Using 'the Personal' to Recover[y] an Essential[ist] Tension in Academic Discourse. *College English* 64: 88–108.

———, ed. 2001. Personal Writing. Special focus, College English 64, no. 1.

———, ed. 2003. The Personal in Academic Writing. Special issue, *College English* 66, no. 1.

Hirsch, E.D., Jr. 1977. *The Philosophy of Composition.* Chicago: Univ. of Chicago Press.

Hopper, Paul J. Emergent Grammar. 1988. In *The New Psychology of Language: Cognitive and Functional Approaches to Language Structure.* Ed. Michael Tomasello. Mahwah, NJ: Lawrence Erlbaum. 155–75.

Horner, Bruce. 1994. Resisting Traditions in Composing Composition. *JAC: A Journal of Composition Theory* 14: 495–519.

Hunt, Kellogg W. 1965. A Synopsis of Clause-to-Sentence Length Factors. *English Journal* 54: 300; 305–09.

Innes, Doreen C., ed. and trans. 1995. Introd. to *On Style*, by Demetrius. Cambridge, MA: Harvard Univ. Press. 311–42.

Isocrates. 1929. Against the Sophists. *Isocrates*. Vol. 2. Trans. George Norlin. Cambridge, MA: Harvard Univ. Press. 162–77.

Jakobson, Roman. 1960. Concluding Statement: Linguistics and Poetics. In *Style in Language*. Ed. Thomas Sebeok, 350–77. Cambridge, MA: MIT.

Jarratt, Susan. 2003. Rhetoric in Crisis?: The View from Here. *Enculturation* 5.1 (Fall). http://enculturation.gmu.edu/5.1/jarratt.html (accessed May 25, 2007).

Jasinski, James. 2001. Style. In *Sourcebook on Rhetoric*. Thousand Oaks, CA: Sage. 536–59.

Johnson, T. R. 2003. *A Rhetoric of Pleasure: Prose Style and Today's Composition Classroom*. Portsmouth, NH: Heinemann-Boynton/Cook.

Johnson, T. R., and Tom Pace. 2005. *Refiguring Prose Style: Possibilities for Writing Pedagogy*. Logan: Utah State Univ. Press.

Joos, Martin. 1962. *The Five Clocks*. Bloomington: Indiana Univ. Research Center in Anthropology, Folklore, and Linguistics.

Katula, Gary. 1995. Commentary: Lysias, On the Refusal of a Pension to the Invalid. In Murphy and Katula 1995, 228–31.

Kelly, Douglas. 1978. Topical Invention in Medieval French Literature. In *Medieval Eloquence: Studies in the Theory and Practice of Medieval Rhetoric*. Ed. James J. Murphy, 231–51. Berkeley: Univ. of California Press.

Kennedy, George A. 1999. *Classical Rhetoric and Its Christian and Secular Tradition: From Ancient to Modern Times*. 2nd ed. Rev. and enlarged. Chapel Hill: Univ. of North Carolina Press.

Kennedy, Mary Lynch, ed. 1998. *Theorizing Composition: A Critical Sourcebook of Theory and Scholarship in Contemporary Composition Studies*. Westport, CT: Greenwood.

Kinneavy, James. 1971. *A Theory of Discourse: The Aims of Discourse*. Englewood Cliffs, NJ: Prentice-Hall.

Kolln, Martha. 1999. Cohesion and Coherence. In *Evaluating Writing: The Role of Teachers' Knowledge about Text, Learning, and Culture*. Ed. Charles R. Cooper and Lee Odell, 93–113. Urbana, IL: NCTE.

———. 2007. *Rhetorical Grammar: Grammatical Choices, Rhetorical Effects*. 5th ed. New York: Longman.

Laib, Nevin. 1990. Conciseness and Amplification. *College Composition and Communication* 41: 443–59.

Lanham, Richard A. 1974 *Style: An Anti-Textbook*. New Haven, CT: Yale Univ. Press.

———. 1976. *The Motives of Eloquence: Literary Rhetoric in the Renaissance*. New Haven: Yale Univ. Press.

———. 1983a. *Analyzing Prose*. New York: Charles Scribner's Sons.

———. 1983b. *Literacy and the Survival of Humanism*. New Haven, CT: Yale Univ. Press.

———. 1993. *The Electronic Word: Democracy, Technology, and the Arts*. Chicago: Univ. of Chicago Press.

———. 2006. *The Economics of Attention: Style and Substance in the Age of Information*. Chicago: Univ. of Chicago Press.

Larson, Richard. 1976. Structure and Form in Non-Fiction Prose. In Tate 1976, 45–71.

Lauer, Janice. 2002. Rhetorical Invention: The Diaspora. In Atwill and Lauer 2002, 1–15.

Lim, Shirley Geok-lin. 1996. *Among the White Moon Faces: An Asian-American Memoir of Homelands.* New York: Feminist Press.

Little, Greta. Punctuation. 1984. In Moran and Lunsford 1984, 371–98.

Love, Glen A., and Michael Payne. 1969. *Contemporary Essays on Style: Rhetoric, Linguistics, and Criticism.* Glenview, IL: Scott, Foresman.

Lysias. 1967. *Lysias.* Trans. W. R. M. Lamb. Cambridge, MA: Harvard Univ. Press.

Mac Donald, Heather. 1995. Why Johnny Can't Write. *The Public Interest* 120: 3–13. http://Search.ebscohost.com/login.aspx?direct=true&db=aph&AN=9510086540&site=ehost–live (accessed June 12, 2007).

MacDonald, Susan Peck. 2007. The Erasure of Language. *College Composition and Communication* 58: 585–625.

Mann, Nancy. 2003. Point Counterpoint: Teaching Punctuation as Information Management. *College Composition and Communication* 54: 359–93.

Mathieu, Paula. 2005. *Tactics of Hope: The Public Turn in English Composition.* Portsmouth, NH: Heinemann Boynton/Cook.

McComiskey, Bruce. 2000. *Teaching Composition as a Social Process.* Logan: Utah State Univ. Press.

McQuade, Donald A., ed. 1979. *Linguistics, Stylistics, and the Teaching of Composition.* Studies in Contemporary Language #2. Akron: Univ. of Akron Department of English.

———. 1986. *The Territory of Language: Linguistics, Stylistics, and the Teaching of Composition.* Carbondale: Southern Illinois Univ. Press.

Mellon, John C. 1969. *Transformational Sentence Combining: A Method for Enhancing the Development of Syntactic Fluency in English Composition.* Urbana, IL: NCTE.

———.1979. Issues in the Theory and Practice of Sentence Combining: A Twenty Year Perspective. In *Sentence Combining and the Teaching of Writing.* Ed. Donald A. Daiker, Andrew Kerek, and Max Morenberg, 1–38. Akron: University of Akron Department of English

Menand. Louis. 2000. Comp Time: Is College Too Late to Learn How to Write? *The New Yorker* 11 Sept. 92–94.

Micciche, Laura R. 2004. Making the Case for Rhetorical Grammar. *College Composition and Communication* 55: 716–37.

Milic, Louis T. 1965. Theories of Style and Their Implications for the Teaching of Composition. *College Composition and Communication* 16: 66–69; 126.

———. 1971. Rhetorical Choice and Stylistic Option: The Conscious and Unconscious Poles. In Chatman 1971, 77–88.

———. 1975. The Problem of Style. In Winterowd 1975, 271–95.

———. 1986. Composition via Stylistics. In McQuade 1986, 192–203.

Miller, Carolyn R. 1984. Genre as Social Action. *Quarterly Journal of Speech* 70: 151–67.

Miller, Susan. 1991. *Textual Carnivals: The Politics of Composition.* Carbondale: Southern Illinois Univ. Press.

Minock, Mary. 1995. Toward a Postmodern Pedagogy of Imitation. *JAC: A Journal of Composition Theory* 15: 489–509.

Moffett, James. 1968. *Teaching the Universe of Discourse.* Portsmouth, NH: Heinemann-Boynton/Cook.

Moran, Mary Hurley. 1984. Vocabulary Development. In Moran and Lunsford 1984, 347–70.

Moran, Michael G., and Ronald F. Lunsford, eds. 1984. *Research in Composition and Rhetoric: A Bibliographic Sourcebook.* Westport, CT: Greenwood.

Morris, Edmund. 1999. *Dutch: A Memoir of Ronald Reagan.* New York: Random House.

Mulroy, David. 2003. *The War against Grammar.* Portsmouth, NH: Boynton/Cook.

Murphy, James J. 2001. The Key Role of Habit in Roman Writing Instruction. In Murphy 2001. 35–78.

———, ed. 2001. *A Short History of Writing Instruction: From Ancient Greece to Modern America.* 2nd ed. Davis, CA: Hermagoras/LEA.

Murphy, James J., and Richard A. Katula, eds. 1995. *A Synoptic History of Classical Rhetoric.* 2nd ed. Davis, CA: Hermagoras.

Myers, Sharon A. 2003. ReMembering the Sentence. *College Composition and Communication* 54: 610–28.

Neel, Jasper. 1988. *Plato, Derrida, and Writing.* Carbondale: Southern Illinois Univ. Press.

O'Hare, Frank. 1973. *Sentence Combining: Improving Student Writing without Formal Grammar Instruction.* Urbana, IL: NCTE.

Ohmann, Richard. 1959. Prolegomena to the Analysis of Prose Style. In *Style in Prose Fiction: English Institute Essays, 1958.* Ed. Harold C. Martin, 1–24. New York: Columbia Univ. Press.

———. 1967. Generative Grammars and the Concept of Literary Style. In Steinmann 1967, 134–60.

Ong, Walter J. 1974. *Ramus, Method, and the Decay of Dialogue.* New York: Octagon.

———. 1982. *Orality and Literacy: Technologizing the Word.* London: Methuen.

Ostrom, Hans. 1997. Grammar J, As in Jazzing Around: The Roles 'Play' Plays in Style. In Bishop 1997, 75–87.

Pace, Tom. 2005. Style and the Renaissance of Composition Studies. In Johnson and Pace 2005, 3–22.

Pagnol, Marcel. 1960. *My Father's Glory and My Mother's Castle: Memories of Childhood.* Trans. Rita Barisse. New York: North Point/Farrar, Straus and Giroux.

Perelman, Chaïm. 1979. *The New Rhetoric and the Humanities: Essays on Rhetoric and Its Applications.* Dordrecht, Holland: D. Reidel.

Phelps, Louise Wetherbee. 1984. Cross-Sections in an Emerging Psychology of Composition. In Moran and Lunsford 1984, 27–69.

———.1988. *Composition as a Human Science: Contributions to the Self-Understanding of a Discipline.* New York: Oxford Univ. Press.

———. 1999. Paths Not Taken: Recovering History as Alternate Future. In Rosner, Boehm, and Journet 1999, 39–58.

Plato. 1914. Phaedrus. In *Plato.* Vol. 1. Trans. Harold North Fowler. Cambridge, MA: Harvard Univ. Press. 412–579.

———. 1925. Gorgias. In *Plato.* Vol. 5. Trans. W. R. M. Lamb. Cambridge, MA: Harvard Univ. Press. 258–533.

Pooley, Robert C. 1976. *The Teaching of English Usage.* 2nd ed. Chicago: NCTE.

Posner, Richard A. 2001. *Public Intellectuals: A Study of Decline.* Cambridge, MA: Harvard Univ. Press.

Pratt, Mary Louise. 1977. *Toward a Speech Act Theory of Literary Discourse.* Bloomington: Indiana Univ. Press.

Proust, Marcel. 1981. *Remembrance of Things Past.* Trans. C. K. Scott Moncrieff and Terence Kilmartin. New York: Vintage.

Quintilian. 1953. *Institutio Oratoria.* Trans. H. E. Butler. Vol. 3, bk. 7–9. Cambridge, MA: Harvard Univ. Press.

Ramus, Peter. 1986. Arguments in Rhetoric against Quintilian. In *Arguments in Rhetoric against Quintilian: Translation and Text of Peter Ramus's* Rhetoricae Dinstinctiones in Quintilianum. Ed. James J. Murphy. Trans. Carole Newlands. Carbondale: Southern Illinois Univ. Press.

Rankin, Elizabeth D. 1985. Revitalizing Style: Toward a New Theory and Pedagogy. *Freshman English News* 14: 8–13.

Read, Charles. 1971. Pre-School Children's Knowledge of English Phonology. *Harvard Educational Review* 41: 1–34.

Reedy, Jeremiah. 2003. Rev. of *The War Against Grammar,* by David Mulroy. *Bryn Mawr Classical Review* 12: 15.

Rhetorica ad Herennium. 1954. Trans. Harry Caplan. Cambridge, MA: Harvard Univ. Press.

Riley, Kathryn, and Frank Parker. 1998. *English Grammar: Prescriptive, Descriptive, Generative, Performance.* Boston: Allyn and Bacon.

Rodgers, Paul C. 1966. Symposium on the Paragraph. With William F. Irmscher, Francis Christensen, A. L. Becker, Josephine Miles, and David H. Karrfalt. *College Composition and Communication* 17: 60–87.

Roen, Duane. 1996. Discourse Analysis. In T. Enos 1996, 193.

Rose, Mike. 1989. *Lives on the Boundary: The Struggles and Achievement of America's Underprepared.* New York: Free Press.

Rose, Shirley K. 1983. Down from the Haymow: One Hundred Years of Sentence-Combining. *College English* 45: 483–91.

Rosner, Mary, Beth Boehm, and Debra Journet, eds. *History, Reflection, and Narrative: The Professionalization of Composition, 1963–1983.* Stamford, CT: Ablex.

Royster, Jacqueline Jones. 2000. *Traces of a Stream: Literacy and Social Change among African American Women.* Pittsburgh: Univ. of Pittsburgh Press.

Safire, William. 1999. On Language. *New York Times Magazine* 4 Apr.: 37.

Schroeder, Christopher, Helen Fox, and Patricia Bizzell, eds. 2002. *Alt Dis: Alternative Discourses and the Academy.* Portsmouth, NH: Heinemann-Boynton/Cook.

Smit, David W. 2004. *The End of Composition Studies.* Carbondale: Southern Illinois Univ. Press.

Sokal, Alan. 1996a. Transgressing the Boundaries: Toward a Transformative Hermeneutics of Quantum Gravity. *Social Text* 14: 217–52.

———. 1996b. A Physicist Experiments with Cultural Studies. *Lingua Franca* 6.4: 62–64.

Spencer, Herbert. 1881. The Philosophy of Style. In *Essays, Moral, Political and Aesthetic.* New York: D. Appleton. 9–47.

Steinman, Martin, Jr. 1967. *New Rhetorics*. New York: Charles Scribner's Sons.

Strunk, William, Jr., and E.B. White. 2000. *The Elements of Style*. 4th ed. New York: Longman.

Stull, William L. 1985. Sentence Combining, Generative Rhetoric, and Concepts of Style. In *Sentence Combining: A Rhetorical Perspective*. Ed. Donald A. Daiker, Andrew Kerek, and Max Morenberg. Carbondale: Southern Illinois Univ. Press. 76–85.

Syverson, Margaret A. 1999. *The Wealth of Reality: An Ecology of Composition*. Carbondale: Southern Illinois Univ. Press.

Tate, Gary, ed. 1976. *Teaching Composition: Ten Bibliographic Essays*. Fort Worth, TX: Texas Christian Univ. Press.

———. 1987. *Teaching Composition: Twelve Bibliographic Essays*. Forth Worth, TX: Texas Christian Univ. Press.

Taylor, Mary Vaiana. 1975. The Folklore of Usage. In *Ideas for English 101: Teaching Writing in College*. Ed. Richard Ohmann and W.B. Coley. Urbana, IL: NCTE. 205–16.

Tobin, Lad. 1994. Introduction: How the Writing Process Was Born—And Other Conversion Narratives. In Tobin and Newkirk 1994, 1–14.

———. 1997. The Case for Double-Voiced Discourse. In Bishop 1997, 44–53.

Tobin, Lad, and Thomas Newkirk, eds. 1994. *Taking Stock: The Writing Process Movement in the 90s*. Portsmouth, NH: Boynton/Cook.

Todorov, Tzvetan. 1971. The Place of Style in the Structure of the Text. In Chatman 1971, 29–39.

Tokarczyk, Michelle M., and Irene Papoulis, eds. 2003. *Teaching Composition/Teaching Literature: Crossing Great Divides*. New York: Peter Lang.

Truss, Lynne. 2004. *Eats, Shoots & Leaves: The Zero Tolerance Approach to Punctuation*. New York: Gotham.

Tufte, Virginia. 1971. *Grammar as Style*. New York: Holt, Rhinehart.

Vande Kopple, William J. 1990. Something Old, Something New: Functional Sentence Perspective. *Rhetoric and Composition: A Sourcebook for Teachers and Writers*. 3rd ed. Ed. Richard L. Graves. Portsmouth, NH: Heinemann-Boynton/Cook. 215–28.

Vavra, Linda. 1998. Stylistics. In Kennedy, 1998 314–19.

Vickers, Brian. 1988. *In Defence of Rhetoric*. Oxford: Oxford Univ. Press.

Villanueva, Victor, Jr. 1993. *Bootstraps: From an American Academic of Color*. Urbana, IL: NCTE.

Vitanza, Victor J. 1993. Interview by Cynthia Haynes-Burton. *Composition Studies* 21 49–65.

———. 1994. Reading, Writing, Rambling On. Interview by Cynthia Haynes-Burton. *Harper's*, January 1994: 29.

Vygotsky, Lev. 1997. *Thought and Language*. Ed. and Trans. Alex Kozulin. Cambridge, MA: MIT Press.

Wall, Susan. 1994. Where Your Treasure Is: Accounting for Differences in Our Talk about Teaching. In Tobin and Newkirk 1994, 239–60.

Walker, Alice. 1983. *In Search of Our Mothers' Gardens: Womanist Prose*. New York: Harcourt.

Walpole, Jane R. 1980. Style as Option. *College Composition and Communication* 31: 205–12.

Warner, Michael. 2002. *Publics and Counterpublics.* New York: Zone.

Warnock, John. 1984. The Writing Process. In Moran and Lunsford 1984, 3–26

———. 1996. Process/Product. In Enos 1996, 561.

Weathers, Winston. 1980. *An Alternate Style: Options in Composition.* Rochelle Park, NJ: Hayden.

———. 1981. Teaching Style: A Possible Anatomy. In *The Writing Teacher's Sourcebook.* Ed. Gary Tate and Edward P. J. Corbett, 325–32. New York: Oxford Univ. Press.

———. 1990. Grammars of Style: New Options in Composition. In *Rhetoric and Composition: A Sourcebook for Teachers and Writers,* 3rd ed. Ed. Richard L. Graves, 200–14. Portsmouth, NH: Boynton/Cook-Heinemann.

Weathers, Winston, and Otis Winchester. 1969. *Copy and Compose: A Guide to Prose Style.* Englewood Cliffs, NJ: Prentice-Hall.

Weisser, Christian. 2002. *Moving Beyond Academic Discourse: Composition Studies and the Public Sphere.* Carbondale: Southern Illinois Univ. Press.

Willard-Traub, Margaret K. 2003. Rhetorics of Gender and Ethnicity in Scholarly Memoir: Notes on a Material Genre. *College English* 65: 511–25.

Williams, David R. 2000. *Sin Boldly: Dr. Dave's Guide to Writing the College Paper.* New York: Perseus.

Williams, Joseph M. 1994. *Style: Ten Lessons in Clarity and Grace.* 4th ed. New York: HarperCollins College.

Williams, Joseph M., and Rosemary Hake. 1986. Non-Linguistics Linguistics and the Teaching of Style. In McQuade 1986, 174–91.

Winterowd, W. Ross. 1970. Style: A Matter of Manner. *Quarterly Journal of Speech* 56: 161–67.

———. 1975. *Contemporary Rhetoric: A Conceptual Background with Readings.* New York: Harcourt.

———. 1976. Linguistics and Composition. In Tate 1976, 197–222.

———. 1986. *Dispositio*: The Concept of Form in Discourse. In *Composition/Rhetoric: A Synthesis.* Carbondale: Southern Illinois Univ. Press. 245–52.

———. 1987. Literacy, Linguistics, and Rhetoric. In Tate 1987, 265–90.

Witte, Stephen P., and Lester Faigley. 1997. Coherence, Cohesion, and Writing Quality. In *Cross-Talk in Comp Theory: A Reader.* Ed. Victor Villanueva, Jr. Urbana, IL: NCTE. 213–32.

Yancey, Kathleen Blake. 2006. Grammar Drills Coming Back? WPA-L, October 24, 2006, https: //lists.asu.edu/cgi–bin/wa?A2=ind0610&L=WPA–L&P=R66205&D=0&H=0&O=T&T=1

Young, Richard E. 1976. Invention: A Topographical Survey. In Tate 1976, 1–43.

———. 1978. Paradigms and Problems: Needed Research in Rhetorical Invention. *Research on Composing: Points of Departure.* Ed. Charles R. Cooper and Lee Odell. Urbana, IL: NCTE. 29–47.

Young, Richard E., and Alton L. Becker. 1967. Toward a Modern Theory of Rhetoric: A Tagmemic Contribution. In Steinmann 1967, 77–107.

Young, Richard E., Alton L. Becker, and Kenneth L. Pike. 1970. *Rhetoric: Discovery and Change.* New York: Harcourt.

Zebroski, James T. 1999. The Expressivist Menace. In Rosner, Boehm, and Journet 1999, 99–113.

———. 2005. Theory in the Diaspora. *JAC: A Journal of Composition Theory* 25: 651–82.

Zepernick, Janet. 2005. Grammar or Sentence Pedagogies? WPA-L, June 8, 2005, https:// lists.asu.edu/cgi–bin/wa?A2=ind0506&L=WPA–L&T=0&F=&S=&P=18515.

INDEX

ABOUT THE AUTHOR

Paul Butler is assistant professor of English at the University of Nevada, Reno, where he teaches undergraduate and graduate courses in rhetoric and composition, including composition theory and pedagogy, the craft of writing, research methodologies, and style studies. He is currently coauthoring a textbook on style. His previous articles have appeared in *JAC, Rhetoric Review, WPA: Writing Program Administration, Reflections: Writing, Service-Learning, and Community Literacy,* and *Authorship in Composition Studies.*